Politics and the rise of the press

Historical Connections

Series editors
Tom Scott *University of Liverpool*
Geoffrey Crossick *University of Essex*
John Davis *University of Connecticut*
Joanna Innes *Somerville College, University of Oxford*

Titles in the series

Politics and the rise of the press

Britain and France, 1620–1800

Bob Harris

London and New York

First published 1996
by Routledge
11 New Fetter Lane, London EC4P 4EE

Simultaneously published in the USA and Canada
by Routledge
29 West 35th Street, New York, NY 10001

Routledge is an International Thomson Publishing company

© 1996 Bob Harris

Typeset in Times by Routledge
Printed and bound in Great Britain by Clays Ltd, St Ives PLC

British Library Cataloguing in Publication Data
A catalogue record for this book is available from the British
Library

Library of Congress Cataloguing in Publication Data
Harris, Bob, 1964–
    The press and politics: Britain and France, 1620–1800/Bob
    Harris.
    p. cm. – (Historical connections)
    Includes bibliographical references and index.
    1. Press and politics – Great Britain – History. 2. Press and
    politics – France – History. 3. English newspapers – Great
    Britain – History. 4. French newspapers – France – History. I.
    Title. II. Series.
    PN5124.P6H37 1996
    072–dc20
                                                96-4540
                                                  CIP

ISBN 0–415–12273–2

Contents

Series editors' preface

Historical Connections is a series of short books on important historical topics and debates, written primarily for those studying and teaching history. The books offer original and challenging works of synthesis that will make new themes accessible, or old themes accessible in new ways, build bridges between different chronological periods and different historical debates, and encourage comparative discussion in history.

If the study of history is to remain exciting and creative, then the tendency to fragmentation must be resisted. The inflexibility of older assumptions about the relationship between economic, social, cultural and political history has been exposed by recent historical writing, but the impression has sometimes been left that history is little more than a chapter of accidents. This series insists on the importance of processes of historical change, and it explores the connections within history: connections between different layers and forms of historical experience, as well as connections that resist the fragmentary consequences of new forms of specialism in historical research.

Historical Connections puts the search for these connections back at the top of the agenda by exploring new ways of uniting the different strands of historical experience, and by affirming the importance of studying change and movement in history.

Geoffrey Crossick
John Davis
Joanna Innes
Tom Scott

Acknowledgements

A book of this nature is only possible because of the efforts of other scholars. On the British side, the work of Jeremy Black and Michael Harris has been invaluable. Increasing numbers of scholars are working on the early French press, and the superb collaborative volumes on French journals and journalists of this period edited by Jean Sgard are powerful testimonies to their efforts. I have greatly enjoyed having the excuse to read closely and to use these volumes. I have drawn heavily, as anyone looking at the French press in this period must, on the work of Jeremy Popkin, J.R. Censer, Pierre Rétat and Gilles Feyel. If I have misrepresented their findings, then the fault is entirely my own. All I can do here is record my debt to them.

Early drafts of chapters of this book were read by Jeremy Black and Joanna Innes. As always, their comments have been extremely valuable. Jeremy Black's unfailing generosity and interest have acted as a powerful spur to the production of this book. Another historian who read early drafts, and whose comments have always proved helpful, especially on Scottish questions, is my colleague Chris Whatley. As someone born and educated in England and now working in a Scottish university, I am more acutely aware than ever of the tendency of English historians to ignore or quickly pass over affairs north of the border. I have attempted to write this book from a British perspective. If I have done this with any success, it is owing in no small measure to the help and encouragement that I have received from Chris Whatley.

Introduction

> I believe the people of Great Britain are governed by a power that was never heard of as a supreme authority in any age or country before.... It is the government of the press.
>
> (Joseph Danvers, MP for Totnes, in 1738, quoted in Targett, 1991, p. 6)

The historic importance of the rise of newspaper in England and Scotland has long been recognized. The press has always been a symbol of progress, a symbol of the spread of more open forms of government. For these reasons, it has also always attracted its fair share of historians. In the nineteenth century, a number of individuals sought to plot the emergence by the early nineteenth century of the newspaper into something like its modern, or mature, form. Historians in this century have sought to build on this pioneering work to understand more fully the development of the early English and Scottish press, the economics of press production, the role of printers, publishers and booksellers as well as that most elusive of subjects, the newspaper reader. Others have sought to tell the story, often in heroic terms, of the achievement of press freedom. Political historians, meanwhile, have mined the contents of the press to recover different aspects of political life in early modern Britain, in particular the development of ideologies and the popularity of various political ideas.

This work has added immeasurably to our knowledge of the early press, but many questions remain to be fully answered. How far did the press penetrate the everyday lives of people in different areas of Britain before 1800? How did the press help contemporaries to make sense of politics? How far did the press weld together disparate communities, economies and even nations into a single political unit? What was the relationship between the press and the emergence of a new and increasingly pervasive force in eighteenth-century British politics – public opinion? Much of the existing work also fails to tackle very clearly the issue of how far the newspaper was a distinctive form of communication, different from other aspects of print culture. This reflects a marked tendency to portray the press as essentially a mirror of ideas and attitudes that were present in society. What is often lacking is a sense of the early newspaper as a formative influence in public opinion and in social, economic and cultural life, as an 'active force' in history.

The early French press – the second of the major subjects of this book – has until relatively recently attracted far less attention than its British counterpart. This reflects the traditional perception that politics in France before 1789 was conducted in ways and through structures which provided little or no scope for the intervention of the press. In more recent years, as part of wider reassessment of old-regime politics, French historians have turned again to the press, asking new questions of it, and perceiving in it another way of understanding the changing realities of politics in the eighteenth century. Public opinion and the press have been rediscovered as active participants in French politics and history before 1789. Moreover, while still acknowledging that 1789 represented a fundamental break, more and more historians are now emphasizing the importance of continuities between pre-revolutionary and revolutionary political culture. For some, it is the role of the press that exemplifies these. One of the implications of this is that the contrast between the eighteenth-century British and French press was less stark than has traditionally been supposed.

One of the main aims of this book is to examine such perceptions from a comparative perspective. This has not been done before in any detail. Adopting this approach should allow us to form a clearer judgement about the vitality and influence of the French press under the old regime; it should also allow us to identify very clearly what was distinctive about the British press. This exercise also has a wider historiographical significance. The need for comparative studies in history is increasingly being emphasized. This has special relevance for historians of the eighteenth century. There is a growing recognition that there were many areas of convergence in this period between different countries in Western Europe. There is also a growing awareness of the importance of multiplying interactions between the states of eighteenth-century Europe and their peoples (see esp. Black, 1994a). It is against this changing historiographical background that at least one historian has argued that eighteenth-century Britain shared many of the features that characterized the old regime in Europe and France, that it was, in essence, an old or *ancien* regime (see esp. Clark, 1985). The issues raised by this debate go beyond the scope of this book. The press, however, provides an interesting vehicle for testing at least part of the perception of similarity.

Another of the main aims of this book is to explore the relationships between the rise of the newspaper and changing political, social and cultural realities. It is only relatively recently that historians have begun to face these issues squarely. This is despite the fact that a broad conceptual framework for understanding these relationships has been in existence for over thirty years. The author of this framework is Jürgen Habermas. Habermas argued, in a book first published in German in 1962, that in parallel with major developments in private life in the eighteenth century – associated with economic progress and the growing force of the market – a new political space came into existence (1989). Habermas called this space 'the public sphere'. It was characterized by independence from government and the fact that it was inhabited primarily by members of the bourgeois classes. The press was crucial to its formation and structure; the press was the vehicle by which the private reasonings of bourgeois individuals were rendered public. The public sphere initially emerged as a forum for cultural debate. Public discussion was focused on literary and artistic productions and issues arising from these. Into the space this created, however, politics quickly flowed. The press created a new type of political communication and, with it, a new sort of politics. It was the latter that was institutionalized in Britain, or so Habermas argued, in the changes to the constitution brought about by the 1832 Reform Act.

A number of largely theoretical criticisms have been made of Habermas's theory of the 'public sphere' (see esp. Nathans, 1990). Fewer attempts have been made to test its empirical validity. This book represents such an attempt. Another of the principal themes of the book is therefore the ways in which the rise of the press before 1800 changed political culture and the relationships between this and social, economic and cultural change. I hope in this context not just to make a significant contribution to our understanding of the impact of the early press, but also to perceptions of the political identity and role of the expanding middling ranks, especially in eighteenth-century Britain. Habermas and others have portrayed the rise of the British press in this period as symptomatic of the rise of the middle class. Not only was the press, in this view, an essentially middle-class medium, but it also contributed power-fully, or so it is argued, to the growing political confidence and assertiveness of the middle classes. Political change is thus portrayed as having been basically linear: the rise of the press was a landmark in this process. By encouraging public intervention in politics, the press acted to undermine traditional structures and forms of political life. Under the impact of the press, politics became more open. It also became increasingly shaped by the wishes of the growing middle classes.

The book is divided into four chapters. The first chapter traces the development of the newspaper in Britain from its origins in the 1620s up to 1800. Chapter 2 offers an interpretation of how the expansion of the press, particularly from the later seventeenth century, shaped and transformed political life in Britain. Chapter 3 looks at the French press before 1789 and seeks to compare it to the British press of the same period and also the revolutionary French press. Chapter 4 explores a number of more general questions about the impact of the press on political culture and social and cultural divisions, primarily, although not exclusively, in Britain.

A final word about the subject of this book. This book is about the impact of the newspaper press. It is not about print culture in general. Pamphlets, printed ballads and songs, political prints, handbills and other printed ephemera are not examined in any detail. A common-sense definition of newspapers is adopted here. Newspapers are defined as periodical publications that included regular comment and information on domestic and foreign political events, in which this comprised a substantial proportion of their content, and which appeared at least weekly. Historians have spilt vast quantities of ink in trying to define clearly the differences between various sorts of periodical publication in this period, and no definition is without its problems. Throughout the eighteenth century, there was much overlap between the content of newspapers, periodicals and other forms of printed propaganda. The concentration on the regular dissemination of news is, however, fully justifiable. In so far as we are interested in changes in political culture, the significance of the widespread circulation of news and comment on news and political events was a factor of crucial importance. This perception was not lost on contemporaries. In the 1630s and 1640s, it is striking that most attempts to police the press were aimed at publications carrying news and not propaganda. In Britain at least, the newspaper also became, during the eighteenth century, in many contexts and for many purposes, the most important vehicle for printed political comment. This was not accidental. Where pamphlets, prints, ballads and verses were occasional, the newspaper offered the possibility of continuous communication and commentary on political events. This is not to deny that other forms of print were influential. But it was increasingly through and around the press that public discussion of national politics was organized. This book also represents an interpretation of the political significance of the rise of the British and French press rather than a full guide to its various features. Readers seeking greater details on numbers, titles, print runs, personalities, journalists, the technical aspects of the manufacture of news and the economics of the press should consult the Bibliography. The emphasis here will be on placing the development of the press in an economic and social context and probing the many complex ways in which political culture and life were transformed by its emergence and expansion.

1 News serials, newspapers and their readers in Britain, 1620–1800

This chapter traces the progress of news periodicals and their readership in England and Scotland from the early seventeenth century up to 1800. The bulk of the chapter focuses on the period after 1695, when pre-publication censorship lapsed in England and Wales, and the newspaper finally emerged as a major and continuous feature of national political and cultural life. (In Scotland, pre-publication censorship remained on the statute book but was increasingly ignored from the 1710s.) The first section focuses on the 'prehistory' of the newspaper, and emphasizes the widespread circulation of news, especially in England, from the early seventeenth century. The rapid development of the newspaper after 1695 owed much to progress in the previous seventy years or so, together with steady social and economic change in the same period.

The assumption that news did not circulate widely in Britain before 1695 has proved hard to undermine. Most historians accept that London provided a potentially huge market for news periodicals throughout the seventeenth century. This was partly a function of high levels of literacy in the capital – by the middle of the century around 80 per cent of the male population was literate compared with 30 per cent for the nation as a whole – and partly a consequence of the capital's unusually open and sophisticated political culture (T. Harris, 1987, pp. 27–35). Outside London, however, the picture that is painted is usually of news penetrating either by routes that were socially very selective – manuscript newsletters or 'separates', MPs, judges – or in ways in which the news itself was extremely selective – for example, via proclamations or the pulpit. In the light of recent work, however, important qualifications need to be made to this picture. New research is beginning to suggest that, while London offered a uniquely large market for news (as it continued to do in the eighteenth century), the provincial appetite for news in this period was not insignificant; neither were the means to serve it.

Not surprisingly, it is in periods of political tension and crisis that this has been most fully revealed. Thus, much recent work focuses on the 1620s, a period of interrelated international and domestic political conflict. This decade saw the appearance of the first news periodicals in England – corantos. These were published in London, were usually in quarto format, twenty-four pages in length, and furnished readers with foreign news (for an introduction to these and other forerunners of the newspaper, see Frank, 1961; Schaaber, 1965; Lambert, 1992). One historian has recently asserted that these news serials had 'a widespread national readership' (Frearson, 1993, p. 1). The size of editions was between 250 and 1,500 copies, although we lack any firm figures for this. They were distributed beyond London by various methods, although the most important was the growing number of London carriers. These packhorse drivers and waggoners carried goods, together with corre-spondence before 1635, between the capital and many places in provincial England and even Scotland.

Within local communities in the 1620s, news travelled by a combina-tion of formal and informal means (Cust, 1986). One common starting point was a 'separate', a manuscript account of, for example, parlia-mentary proceedings. Most of these separates were probably purchased by the relatively wealthy. But they appear to have circulated among neighbours and in this way could come into the hands of less wealthy individuals. News from written and other sources also travelled by word of mouth. In 1634, Thomas Cotton read out his weekly London newsletter 'evry markett daye att Colchester', surrounded by listeners 'as people [do] when Ballads are sunge' (quoted in Frearson, 1993, p. 17). A news diary kept by a Suffolk clergyman, John Rous, illustrates how much news could reach even the relatively isolated provincial observer (Cust, 1986). What is interesting about Rous is that he rarely travelled outside his home area. His social contacts were also with individuals of a similar social standing – fellow clergymen, minor gentry and literate yeomen. Rous records having received a few newsletters and corantos from London, but the most commonly cited source of news is local gossip or talk. The content of this talk was broadly similar to reports in contemporary newsletters or 'separates'. What Rous's diary illustrates is the many potential points of contact in early seventeenth-century society both between London and the provinces and within local communities, along which news and news serials could travel.

The model for the dissemination of news that has been uncovered for the 1620s was undoubtedly imitated and extended during the civil wars of the mid-seventeenth century. The wars and political convulsions of the period created a broad-based demand for news, as well as printers and publishers enterprising enough to respond to it. The principal printed forms that news took were diurnals, mercuries, corantos and gazettes, or newsbooks as they have been collectively called by historians (Frank, 1961; Raymond, 1993). These were mostly printed in London. They were weekly publications, usually of eight pages, and had circulations of anything between a few hundred and, on rare occasions, a few thousand. They carried a huge variety of material – political, social, and at times scatalogical. Unlike the corantos of the 1620s, they included news of domestic events and politics. Although Parliament sought to impose controls on them as early as 1643, they were disseminated largely unhindered until Cromwell had them suppressed and strict control of the press was reintroduced in 1654 (Siebert, 1965, pp. 230–2). In Scotland, only a handful of newsbooks appeared during the civil wars and interregnum, and the majority of these appear to have been aimed at English soldiers stationed around Edinburgh. However, William Couper, the early twentieth-century historian of the Edinburgh press, claims that there are references to the circulation of 'News Letters' in Scotland in 1642 (Couper, 1908, vol. ii, pp. 70–3). He also refers to the practice of groups of county magnates combining to hire a writer in Edinburgh to send them weekly intelligence from the Scottish capital. This letter was then passed around in country districts and often copied. Slightly later in the century, a number of burghs seem to have operated a similar system. Glasgow had a correspondent in Edinburgh from 1652. In 1657 the burgh had a journal sent weekly from London (Eyre-Todd, 1931, vol. ii, p. 258). In 1665 Stirling paid an individual 'two shillings sterling weeklie' for a weekly journal, 'as Glasgow and utheris burghs payes' (Couper, 1908, vol. ii, pp. 70–3). Further research will probably show that this sort of arrangement was common to many Scottish burghs and members of the landed elite in this period.

The bulk of work on news and news publications during the later Stuart period has concentrated on London. James Sutherland has recently underlined the importance of the period 1679–82 as a crucial phase in the development of the newspaper (1986). During this period, the period of the Exclusion crisis, the 1662 Licensing Act – and thus pre-publication censorship – lapsed. It was during this short period of relative press freedom that the outline of the form and content that was to characterize the newspaper for most of the rest of the century began to emerge. Forty-odd short-lived newspapers were published in London in these years. Sutherland's study has nothing to say about provincial distribution of these papers, but scattered evidence suggests that, as in the earlier part of the century, this took place on quite a wide scale. The Newcastle treasurer's account books for 1682 record a payment 'as per order' to 'Mrs Maddison, being the news munger' (*Extracts*, 1965, p. 59). Maddison was almost certainly an agent either in London or Newcastle who supplied the corporation with newspapers. In 1685, the Edinburgh town council instructed the town's treasurer to pay Robert Mein, the postmaster, for furnishing 'for the use of the town ... news letters, gazettes, and other news' (Wood and Armet, 1954, p. 152). Recent work on popular politics during the Exclusion crisis, which shows again the readiness and competence with which provincial opinion responded to opportunities to express itself, also strongly suggests that the mechanisms and channels carved out during the 1620s and mid-century were easily revived when political conditions allowed and demanded it (see esp. T. Harris, 1993, pp. 102–8; Jones, 1961, pp. 167–73; Knights, 1994).

The seventeenth-century background to the development of the newspaper is important for a number of reasons. In the first place, as the next chapter will show, it helps us to picture more clearly some of the ways in which the dissemination and availability of news was transformed by the newspaper after 1695. It also places the newspaper's development after 1695 in its proper perspective. What the seventeenth-century record shows is the extent to which the social and economic conditions for the emergence of a lively national press were already in place, certainly in England. These conditions included the massive size of London, together with the high levels of literacy among its population. London remained a leading influence on print culture in Britain until at least the mid-nineteenth century. The development of printing and of news periodicals in the provinces was closely linked to experiences gained in the capital's large market. Other conditions included a developing market economy, improving physical links between London and the provinces (roads and carrying services), growing prosperity just below the level of the elites in society, and growing familiarity with print, particularly in areas and occupations in which people of middling rank were concentrated. Recent revisions by Peter Lindert and Jeffrey Williamson of Gregory King's social table of England and Wales in 1688 only reinforce this point. These show an economy and society with, already by the late seventeenth century, sizeable commercial and manufacturing sectors. As Lindert and Williamson have written, King 'painted a nation consisting of just London and a vast, poor hinterland ... England and Wales were surely more industrial and commercial in King's day than he has led us to believe' (quoted in Crafts, 1985, p. 14).

The progress of the press after 1695 was rapid. New forms of newspaper multiplied. The papers of 1679–82 had been published twice weekly. In 1695 a number of tri-weekly papers emerged. These papers were published on the post days – Tuesdays, Thursdays and Saturdays. In

1696 the first evening paper appeared. The first tri-weekly evening paper emerged in 1715. The first daily paper – the *Daily Courant* – made its appearance on 11 March 1702. The date of the first provincial paper is less certain. The earliest surviving copy of such a paper – the *Bristol Post-Boy* – dates from 1704, but it is likely that the first provincial paper emerged in Norwich in 1701. Readers had to wait much longer for the first Sunday paper – the *British Gazette and Sunday Monitor*. This only appeared in 1779, and was published in defiance of sabbatarian legislation. The *Edinburgh Gazette* was Scotland's first proper newspaper, appearing briefly in 1680 and reappearing in either 1693 or 1699. It was followed in 1696 by the short-lived *Edinburgh Flying Post* and in 1705 by the longer-lasting *Edinburgh Courant* (see Kelsall and Kelsall, 1986).

The balance between different forms of newspaper changed over the course of the eighteenth century. Michael Harris has estimated that in 1746 London had a total of eighteen papers – six weeklies and essay sheets, together with the same number of tri-weeklies and dailies (1987, p. 31). In 1770, there were five dailies, eight tri-weeklies and four weeklies published in the capital. In 1783 the figures are nine dailies and ten bi- or tri-weeklies; by 1790 fourteen dailies, seven tri-weeklies and two weekly papers (Black, 1987a, p. 14). The growing influence of the daily paper reflects, among other things, the impetus to news reporting provided by Parliament's ceding control in 1771 of the press reporting of its proceedings. When Parliament was in session, after 1771 newspapers had access to interesting copy on a daily basis.

Before 1714, it was the tri-weekly papers that were circulated in greatest number (Price, 1958). Figures based on returns from payment of stamp duty – an impost levied on news-carrying publications from 1712 – show that the *Post-Man*, the most successful paper during Queen Anne's reign, had an average circulation between August and September 1712 of 3,812. The one daily paper of that period – the *Daily Courant* – had average sales of 859 (Snyder, 1968). For about twenty years after 1714, it was the weekly journals and tri-weekly evening papers that proved the most successful. In the early 1720s, before it was purchased by the ministry, the weekly *London Journal* was probably selling around 10,000 copies per issue (M. Harris, 1987, p. 39). By the end of the 1720s, the print run of the most famous political essay paper of the early Hanoverian period – the *Craftsman* – was over 10,000 (Harris, 1970). The most successful tri-weekly evening paper of the same period was almost certainly the *London Evening Post*. This probably had a print run in the mid-century of around 5,000 (M. Harris, 1987, p. 56). These sorts of magnitude of circulation were not exceeded before the early nineteenth century. In 1769 the publication of the famous 'Junius' letters in the influential daily the *Public Advertiser* boosted its circulation from an average of around 2,800 to 3,400 (Brewer, 1976, pp. 143–4). Among many provincial papers there was probably some increase in circulation during the second half of the eighteenth century, although firm evidence for this is slim. Isaac Thompson of the *Newcastle Journal* was claiming 2,000 regular purchasers in 1739, while *Whitworth's Manchester Magazine* boasted that it had a sale of 1,200 in 1755. Many provincial papers before 1750 probably had significantly lower circulations, however, of the order of a few hundred (Cranfield, 1962, pp. 168–76; see also Maxted, 1990). For the second half of the eighteenth century, account books and records survive for a few years for the *Hampshire Chronicle* (Ferdinand, 1990). These provide precise figures for printing, circulation and returns between 1781 and 1783. They show an average print run of around 1,050–1,100. In 1779 the circulation was 500. In 1780 the proprietors of the *Salisbury Journal* were claiming a circulation of 'upwards of 4000' (Ferdinand, 1990). Not all provincial papers were so successful. As late as 1837 the *Devonshire Chronicle* had a circulation of only 250. The circulation of Scottish papers is largely unknown. *Ruddiman's Weekly Magazine* claimed a circulation of 3,000 in the late 1770s (Fagerstrom, 1951, p. 189). If this was true, and Hugo Arnot, the eighteenth-century historian of Edinburgh, also emphasizes the 'unprecedented' nature of the paper's success (Arnot, 1779, p. 453), it perhaps suggests circulations in the hundreds for most eighteenth-century Scottish papers. A claim in 1815 that the two contemporary Aberdeen papers had a combined circulation of 2,000 suggests that this sort of magnitude is probably correct (Wilson, 1822, p. 169).

The growth, therefore, of the eighteenth-century press was not achieved by expanding significantly the circulation of individual newspapers. Instead, the number of titles published multiplied as the century progressed and, with it, the overall circulation of newspapers. The pattern of growth was uneven. The press grew strongly in periods of war and political excitement – most obviously, the 1710s, later 1730s, 1745–6, mid-1750s, later 1760s and early 1770s, later 1770s and early 1780s, and early 1790s – but stagnated or even declined in circulation at other times (Harris, 1978a, p. 88). The general sorts of magnitude involved can be deduced from figures derived from stamp tax records and estimates based on extrapolations from the few figures recorded elsewhere. These should be treated with caution. Stamp tax records are incomplete; they also only survive for certain years. Other figures are often derived from claims made by individuals with an interest in exaggerating circulations. The figures for the stamp tax for 1712 and 1713, the only figures for the first half of the century, are particularly problematic. Nevertheless, from them it has been suggested that in 1713 the annual sale of newspapers was around 2.5 million (Snyder, 1968). In 1750, the date of the next set of surviving stamp tax returns, 7.3 million stamps were purchased by the press. By 1760 the figure had risen to 9.4 million, by 1775 to 12.6 million. Seven million stamps were issued for London papers in 1801, and 9 million for provincial papers. The underlying pattern of growth that emerges therefore is of rapid growth up to 1750, slower growth until around 1780 and then another take-off into much quicker growth after that date.

The patterns of growth revealed by the provincial press and the Scottish press diverge from the general picture. The provincial press grew rapidly between around 1720 and 1750, stagnated until the later 1770s, and then resumed a rapid upwards trend. In 1745 there had been around forty provincial papers. In 1753 the figure fell to thirty-two. By 1782 there were approximately fifty. By 1800 there were over a hundred (Read, 1961, p. 59). The picture for Scotland is necessarily more tentative, since we still lack a modern study of the early Scottish press. Edinburgh and Glasgow dominated Scottish newspaper publishing throughout the eighteenth century. Growth was generally much slower north of the border than in England. But the 1770s and 1780s were something of a turning point. The American war and the war against revolutionary France both gave important boosts to the Scottish press, although the dominance of the two major cities was only reinforced (Craig, 1931; Couper, 1908; Cowan, 1946). This reflected the wide circulation of Edinburgh and Glasgow papers. Elsewhere, papers generally failed to establish a foothold, although by 1800 the two cities had been joined by Aberdeen, Dumfries and Kelso. Dundee, Perth, Berwick, Montrose and Arbroath had also seen the brief appearance of magazine-type periodical publications (see esp. Carnie, n.d.).

Establishing the basic facts surrounding the growth of the press in the eighteenth century is relatively easy. Interpreting these facts is more difficult. Jeremy Black, while acknowledging the extent of the developments that did take place, has recently suggested that the market for the press was more limited than rehearsing figures for overall growth alone would appear to indicate (see esp. Black, 1987a, p. 21). His argument rests on two principal factors. First, many more newspapers failed than succeeded in the eighteenth century. This was true of all forms of paper – London and provincial, weekly, tri-weekly and daily. Over half of the provincial papers published before 1760 failed in the first five years (Wiles, 1965, p. 25). Second, the pattern of growth of the provincial press was uneven (see Wiles, 1965). In some towns, the picture is one of continual innovation and steady expansion. In Manchester, before 1760 six papers came into existence, four of them lasting for more than five years. In the 1740s, Newcastle and the surrounding region was able to support three papers – the *Newcastle Journal*, the *Newcastle Courant* and the *Newcastle Gazette*. Some large and growing towns, however, struggled to support a newspaper until comparatively late. The first Liverpool paper, the *Leverpoole Courant*, appeared in 1713, but only survived for a few issues. It was only in the later 1750s that renewed (and more successful) attempts were made to establish a paper in the city. Third, by comparison with growth in readership in the nineteenth century, the advances of the eighteenth century can be made to seem small. This perception also informs Arthur Aspinall's seminal, albeit now dated, study of the London press between 1780 and 1850. Impressed by the large circulations achieved by certain papers after 1814, when *The Times* started to be produced on a steam-powered press, Aspinall was dismissive of the efforts of eighteenth-century newspaper printers. As he remarked (1949, p. 379):

When Pitt [the Younger] was in Downing Street a newspaper was merely a small commercial speculation designed primarily to advertise new books, quack medicines, theatre programmes, auction sales and shipping news. It contained only a few paragraphs of news and no leading articles; and its sale was measured by hundreds.

The print runs of newspapers during the eighteenth century were certainly circumscribed by various factors. These included technology, cost, content and, to a lesser degree, illiteracy and poor communications. The basic form of technology, the hand-press, made it very difficult to increase print runs above around 1,000 without adding further presses and workmen, something that only a printer sure of future success could contemplate (for the wooden hand-press and the constraints it imposed on newspaper production, see esp. Popkin, 1989, ch. 5).

The relative unimportance of illiteracy is suggested in the first place by the fact that demand for printed material other than newspapers among the lower ranks – for example, almanacs and chapbooks – was generally buoyant throughout the century. As Tessa Watt has argued recently, even in the sixteenth century, rural as well as urban communities were becoming increasingly habituated to literate as well as oral modes of communication (1991). Margaret Spufford has uncovered a massive popular printing industry in the later seventeenth century. Charles Tias, a contemporary London Bridge wholesaler had a stock at his death (in 1664) which included 90,000 chapbooks, that is one for every fifteen families in England and Wales. He also held over 37,000 ballad sheets

(Spufford, 1985, pp. 92–4). The problem for newspaper printers, in other words, was not, in Roger Chartier's phrase, one of 'typographic acculturation' (Chartier, 1989). There was a popular or mass demand for print. The issue, however, was one of whether eighteenth-century newspapers could or did seek to tap it.

The impact of poor communications was uneven and diminished as the century progressed. Communications improved considerably in the course of the century, becoming more extensive, faster and cheaper. The road system was extended and significantly improved by the turnpike revolution of the central decades of the eighteenth century (Pawson, 1977). Journey times were progressively and substantially reduced as a result. More important for the press than better road travel, however, were the knock-on effects that this had on postal services and carrying services (Harris, 1978a, p. 89). Ralph Allen introduced an increasing number of daily postal services in the mid-century, linking London to most parts of England. He was also the driving force behind an increase in the number of cross-posts between provincial towns. The result was, as John Brewer has observed, that by the accession of George III 'most of the major towns in the country were linked both with London and each other by an efficient, frequent daily service' (1976, p. 159). Improvements to the postal service created new opportunities for newspaper printers. Faster communications with London reduced the inherent weakness of weekly publication – the relative tardiness of coverage – and also gave new papers certain advantages over potential rivals further away from the point of sale or readership. The founding of the *Edinburgh Advertiser* in 1764, for example, followed the increase in the previous year of the number of posts between London and Edinburgh from three to five a week.

It was also through the postal service that London papers reached the provinces in growing numbers as the century progressed. The cost of distribution by this route was lowered over time through the franking system, a system whereby certain specified, or franked, items were allowed to pass through the post free of charge (Ellis, 1958, pp. 47–59; Harris, 1978a, pp. 89–90; M. Harris, 1987, pp. 42–6). Before the early 1760s, the privilege of franking rested with the office of the secretaries of state, the six Clerks of the Road, and Members of Parliament. The Clerks used their privilege to operate a profitable newspaper distribution business, charging customers less than the full price for the carriage of newspapers. In the early 1760s, commercial concerns, or private individuals, whose names were registered at the post office, were also given permission to make use of the MPs' privilege. This had the effect of removing the dependency of publishers and printers on the Clerks for cheap distribution; it was also a change that, by further reducing the cost of receiving a London newspaper in the provinces, significantly boosted the distribution of London newspapers through the post office. In 1764, a little fewer than 1.1 million London newspapers were distributed this way. By 1782 the figure had climbed to over 3 million, while at the beginning of the following decade it stood at over 4.5 million. Scottish papers were also largely disseminated through an increasingly extensive postal system (Haldane, 1971, pp. 166–70). English provincial newspapers were less reliant on the postal system. The mainstay of their distribution systems were news agents and specialised news men (Cranfield, 1962, pp. 190–206; Ferdinand, 1990).

This leaves the important factors of cost and content. That cost served seriously to restrict circulation seems indisputable. The motives behind taxing newspapers were both fiscal and political, although the balance between the two was different at various points during the century. Newspaper stamp duty was introduced in 1712 by the Tory ministry of Lord Harley (Downie, 1981; Gibbs, 1992, pp. 240–1). The regulations were tightened up in 1725, while the rate was further increased in 1757, 1776, 1789 and 1797. The increased costs associated with all of these moves were immediately passed on to readers by the newspapers. In 1725 newspapers cost 2d. In 1757 the price rose to 2½d; in 1776 to 3d; in 1789 to 3½d; in 1792 to 4d; and finally to 6d in 1797. In the later eighteenth century, both Lord North and William Pitt the Younger expressed the view that newspapers were luxuries and should be made relatively expensive (Aspinall, 1949, p. 9). The result was that newspapers probably fell outside the purchasing capacity of all those below the skilled working classes, in other words a majority of the population (Black, 1987a, pp. 106–7). If we were able to plot newspaper purchase against a map of society, the numerical preponderance of purchasers would almost certainly fall among the middling ranks or middle classes, a layer of society that encompassed farmers, smaller freeholders, manufacturers, merchants, professionals, tradesmen and shopkeepers. The precise boundaries demarcating this section of society are debated among historians, but none would deny that they were growing in numbers and prosperity particularly after the mid-century, a fact that, as is made clear below, was of enormous importance for the expansion of the press.

That the potential market for newspapers might have been considerably greater had costs been lower seems to be confirmed by the emergence and brief flourishing of a cheap and unstamped press in London in the 1730s and 1740s. As Michael Harris has shown, this shadowy press seems to have operated on a considerable scale (1987, pp. 27–8). One contemporary estimate put the weekly circulation of unstamped papers, which sold at ¼d, at 50,000. Legitimate cut-price tri-weeklies costing 1½d probably reached a circulation of around a few thousand. The unstamped press was suppressed in 1743; the cheap legitimate papers also began to disappear at the same time (Harris, 1987, pp. 29-30). The reasons for this remain unclear. Michael Harris has argued that both developments were 'symptoms of the capture of the London press by the interests of commerce and politics' (1987, p. 195). They reflected, in other words, a growing alliance between the political authorities and strengthening vested interests in the upper reaches of the press. Perhaps unsurprisingly, there is little direct evidence to support this. Harris's argument rests on his contention that newspaper production in London was increasingly dominated in the 1730s and 1740s by congeries of respectable booksellers. Karl Winkler, however, has disputed the existence of any general trend towards greater bookseller ownership of the press in the early Hanoverian period (Winkler, 1988). It is also worth noting that whatever hostility did exist towards new entrants into the market, this did not prevent new papers emerging when political and international circumstances were favourable – for example, in the later 1750s and the later 1760s (Peters, 1980; Brewer, 1976).

The content of the cheap and unstamped papers perhaps provides another clue as to why the legitimate papers never achieved a mass circulation. These papers included material that was aimed at a popular audience – for example, trials of notorious criminals and accounts of murders. By comparison, the vast majority of legitimate and normal-priced newspapers appears to have been written for a readership who followed domestic and international events closely, who could recognize leading political and social personalities through allusions and innuendoes, and who boasted at least some familiarity with classical literature and history. This is an aspect of newspapers that requires further investigation. Contemporary comments are often unhelpful or potentially misleading. These were usually hostile. News writers were often denigrated for their lack of education, their slight hold on polite or high culture. Some of the most scathing comments were reserved for Sir Robert Walpole's hired political writers in the 1730s – William Arnall, James Pitt and Ralph Courteville. Arnall and his fellow ministerial writers were uniformly ridiculed in the opposition press for their low social status and their tenuous hold on high culture. As Simon Targett has argued, such comments are misleading (Targett, 1989). All were skilled writers with considerable education. Newspapers appear to have expected the close and continuous attention of their readers. For most of the century, the organization of news was fairly rudimentary. There was widespread experimentation with headlines and different sizes of type to highlight important pieces of news, particularly from the mid-century. But it was only towards the end of the century that the use of such devices, together with nascent editorials, reached a state of any maturity. Even by the end of the century, however, the detail can often appear overwhelming to a modern reader. The *Edinburgh Weekly Journal*, which first appeared at the beginning of January 1798, felt it necessary to include a summary of foreign affairs in its first issue to help its new readers. As the paper commented (3 January 1798):

> To many of our country readers, who may have had but casual opportunities of consulting newspapers for some time past, an introduction to this department [foreign intelligence] of our paper seems necessary, to enable them to comprehend, and follow us in the details we shall afterwards have to submit to their perusal.

This feature of eighteenth-century newspapers, the assumptions that they made about close familiarity with events and personalities, is one that is often overlooked by historians.

One of the more important reasons for this may be that it seems hard to reconcile with the many comments made throughout the century about the low social status of many newspaper readers. The bulk of the comment about newspaper readership in the eighteenth century that is usually quoted by historians refers to London. It is also often hostile in intent; it is concerned to emphasize the ways in which the press appeared to threaten the political rule of property. As such, it focuses on the collective readership of newspapers, the readership of papers in coffee houses and taverns, the reading out aloud of newspapers, especially by those of comparatively unelevated social status – shopkeepers, artisans and tradesmen. Partly because of the dense network of coffee houses and clubs, artisans and even those a little below artisanal status clearly did have access to newspapers in London and in other large towns. Their readership of newspapers was a fact of some political and social significance, not least because of the size of London's artisanal and luxury economy. But what such comments by design do not draw attention to is the extent to which probably a majority of regular newspaper readers in the capital were members of the upper and middling ranks. The political culture of the coffee house embraced a wide cross-section of society. Describing it as 'popular', certainly before the 1790s, can be misleading if we are assuming that it did not include a sizeable element of people from the upper and middling ranks. Perhaps the dominant feature of coffee houses was the mixed social character of their users. Many coffee houses were associated with groups of merchants. American merchants met at the Pennsylvania, New England,

Carolina and New York coffee houses, all of which appear to have been established in the early 1700s (Olson, 1979–80, p. 35). As the diaries of the first Earl of Egmont indicate, members of the gentry often frequented coffee houses (*Manuscripts*, 1920–3, vol. iii, pp. 2, 42, 260). In the 1760s, the Newcastle Whigs met at Arthur's Coffee House (Brewer, 1976, p. 149). As is the case today, MPs were some of the most avid newspaper readers (see R. Harris, 1993, pp. 34–5). James Boswell often took his breakfast at a coffee house. As he wrote in his journal for 27 November 1762, 'I then breakfasted at Child's Coffee-house, read the political papers, and had some chat with citizens' (Pottle, 1951, p. 51).

Individual purchase of London newspapers, which usually disappears from historical view, was probably concentrated quite high up the social ladder. This is particularly the case in the first half of the eighteenth century. The early development of the *Craftsman*, the most famous political essay paper of the early Hanoverian period, is instructive in this context. The paper began as a single-sheet essay paper with no news content. But it rapidly changed its format and title. It started carrying news; the title became the *Craftsman, or the Country Gazette*. One of the reasons for the change seems to have been its dependence on a readership among those classes of people who formed the heart of the London season. There was a need to retain their readership during the summer months, when they were not resident in the capital. Some thirty years later, the sales of the *Public Advertiser* continued to display a marked seasonal character. As John Brewer has noted, sales reached a peak in February or March, often coinciding with the ending of Parliament (1976, p. 143). They only picked up again in late October or early November with the beginning of a new parliamentary session. The *London Evening Post*, often cited as a 'popular' and in some cases 'populist' early Hanoverian newspaper, appears to have had two different sorts of readership – a socially broad-based London readership and a rather more socially elevated provincial readership. The advertisements carried in the paper were generally aimed at the well-off, being dominated by property (Walker, 1973). Probably fairly representative of the paper's provincial readership, in terms of social standing, were Tory clergy and gentry. In the early 1750s, the cathedral chapter at Durham were arguing about whether to continue subscribing to the paper (Hughes, 1956, pp. 159–60).

Our picture of provincial newspaper readers, particularly in the second half of the eighteenth century, is generally much less clear than of metropolitan readers. The development of provincial newspaper readership has often been portrayed, like that of London readers, primarily in terms of expansion and social deepening (see esp. Money,

1977, pp. 57–79; Brewer, 1976, esp. pp. 143–6). In some towns, for example, Bristol, Norwich, Newcastle, Birmingham and Manchester, such a trend is much more easy to demonstrate than in smaller, less well-known towns, least of all for rural areas. Advertisements show growing numbers of coffee houses in places such as Newcastle and Birmingham stocking large numbers of London as well as provincial papers. As in London, the clientele of these coffee houses undoubtedly stretched into the upper reaches of the lower orders. Yet we should not let our view of provincial newspaper readership become overwhelmed by the historical shadows cast by major towns and cities. The record of provincial papers suggests that the reality was more complex. Even provincial papers published in places such as Newcastle and Manchester still needed to circulate widely on a regional basis to survive and prosper. In 1739, the *Newcastle Journal* cited agents from forty-two towns and villages going as far north as Berwick and as far west as Newhaven. This regionalized pattern of circulation among provincial papers continued in the second half of the eighteenth century, no doubt reinforced by the greater dissemination of London papers outside the metropolitan area (Black, 1987a, pp. 100–1). In 1773 the *Newcastle Journal* was claiming that the circumference of its circulation was now nearly 600 miles. As the number of provincial papers multiplied, as Brewer has observed, 'an increasingly complex, regional network of distribution emerged ... we can be confident that, as the century proceeded, the provincial newspaper was spreading further and further afield' (1976, p. 146). What this means in terms of the social character of readers is much less clear. Alongside greater geographical coverage, it seems likely that certain provincial papers looked to increase their penetration of areas closer to their place of publication as a response to the increased competition. This is certainly the pattern that has been uncovered by Christine Ferdinand in her work on the *Salisbury Journal* (1990). In 1785 the paper had a well-defined area of distribution, 'densely populated' with agents. Forty years previously the number of agents had been far fewer and they had been dispersed throughout a much wider area. It was the steady geographical contraction of the readership of some papers that was to provide the basis for the emergence of a genuinely local press in England in the nineteenth century.

Where in social terms, then, is this expanding readership for provincial papers in the eighteenth century likely to have come from? The advantages of provincial papers for the provincial reader were twofold. They were cheaper, partly because they were weeklies and partly because they avoided the cost of postage; they also contained extracts from all the more important London papers of the preceding week. This may have made them particularly attractive to those who lay outside the highest political and social levels; they were less likely to see the need to consult the London papers regularly. This group probably comprised, at one end of the social scale, the provincial gentry and, at the other end of the social scale, the shopkeeper. The middle elements in this group appear to have comprised the merchants, manufacturers, farmers, smaller freeholders, professionals of various description, and those involved in the distribution and wholesaling trades. As one individual remarked in 1789, 'The source of information to the gentleman farmer and the flourishing manufacturer, who constitute the great body of the free-holders, especially in this county [Yorkshire], is a provincial news-paper' (quoted in Aspinall, 1949, p. 445).

The advertisements in provincial papers offer further clues about their readership. The limitations of this source are fairly obvious. The social terminology employed in many advertisements was not designed to specify the target audience accurately. In a society so driven by the power of social emulation as eighteenth-century Britain, the usual appeal was to snobbery. Gentle status was claimed by a broadening range of groups and occupations (Langford, 1989, pp. 61–121; Corfield, 1987). Other advertisements, for example for personnel such as journeymen or ploughmen, may have been aimed at local notables with knowledge of those needing work rather than those likely to take up the position. A notice published in the *Ipswich Journal* in 1764 by the master tailors of London and Wesminster, assuring journeymen tailors that they would be welcomed in the metropolis, contained the following appeal (22 December 1764): 'The Master-Taylors would be very much obliged to those in whose Hands this Advertisement may come, if they would communicate it to the journeymen of the trade.'

As J.J. Looney has argued, the profile of advertisements, perhaps unsurprisingly, differed between papers and towns and regions (Looney, 1989). Some general patterns, however, do emerge. As far as goods were concerned, luxury goods predominated in all the provincial papers – wines, various textiles, beverages, medicines and books (Black, 1987a, p. 62; Styles, 1993, pp. 541–2). Another important category of advertise-ments was leisure activities – subscription concerts, the theatre, pleasure gardens, walks, assemblies, the races. Not surprisingly, these sorts of advertisement appeared in greatest number in places published in or near to towns with a developed leisure sector – for example, Bath, York and Ipswich. Yet another very important category comprised notices issued by quarter sessions, the lord lieutenancy (often regarding the militia), and the proliferating statutory bodies and voluntary associations of later eighteenth-century England – turnpike commissions, charities, improvement commissions, prosecution associations. In the case of advertisements for leisure activities, such as subscription concerts, it is most likely that, particularly in papers published in or near to so-called leisure towns, they were aimed primarily at visiting and resident gentry and secondarily at the upper reaches of the middling sort – the professionals, the increasingly affluent farmers, the wealthier manufacturers and merchants. Some of the notices provided by semi-official or voluntary bodies would appear to have had a slightly less elevated constituency in mind. The advertisements of prosecution associations are particularly difficult to interpret in this context. These have recently been closely examined by Peter King (1989). The press was used to help organize prosecution associations as well as to advertise their existence and aims. Among the groups that were most disposed to form associations, and mobilize partly through the press, were farmers and smaller freeholders in rural areas, distributors, retailers, and food processors (butchers, bakers, brewers, millers) and manufacturers in urban areas. Once formed, the advertisements issued by prosecution associations often listed the names of members as well as the sorts of crime that they were anxious to punish and reduce. As King has also noted, the efficacy of such threats may be doubted given the opportunist nature of most crime in this period and the limited literacy of those who were responsible for the bulk of it – the labouring classes. Nevertheless, the numbers of prosecution associations advertising by the 1770s and 1780s would seem to indicate that contemporaries perceived a readership for provincial papers that reached quite far down the social scale. The readiness of diverse groups to use the press to launch prosecution associations also suggests a familiarity with the press among members of the the middling orders of quite modest income and status and lacking close links to the landowning classes.

Without new research, it is impossible to say with any great confidence who composed the readership of the Scottish press in the eighteenth century. A few tentative generalizations are possible, however. First, this readership was almost certainly considerably more socially restricted than its English counterpart. This reflected the different social structures of the two countries, the different patterns of urbanization (the major surge in urban growth in Scotland came later than south of the border and was more sharp), and the different shape and timing of economic progress in each. Scottish papers behaved like English provincial papers. Like provincial papers, for example, a major source of competition was the London press. Edinburgh and Glasgow papers had regional circulations. The *Glasgow Mercury* in 1780 included the following notice (10 August 1780):

The subscribers to this paper, who live in the country, and whose papers are become due, will please order payment by any of their correspondents in town. Those in Argyllshire and Western Islands, will pay their accounts to Mr Donald McKenzie, clerk to Messrs. James and Duncan Campbell, merchants in Inverary.

Sixty-five years earlier, the short-lived *Glasgow Courant* had called in its opening number for 'gentlemen' to send news from 'the Towns of Aberdeen, St. Andrews, Inverness, Brechen, Dundee, St. Johnstoun, Stirling, Dumbarton, Inverary, Dumfries, Lanark, Hamiltoun, Renfrew, Paisley, Port Glasgow, Greenock, Irvin, Ayr, Kilmarnock and Stranraer' (Couper, 1908, vol. i, p. 109). There is some evidence that Edinburgh and Glasgow papers penetrated south of the border into the north of England. In early 1783, Richard Townley of Betfield in Lancashire wrote to the *Edinburgh Advertiser* on the subject of the use of grains (3 January 1783). Three overlapping groups appear to have dominated newspaper readership in Scotland for most of the century, certainly before the 1790s – the gentry, local urban elites and merchants. In 1700 Montrose made an arrangement with a minor official at the Edinburgh post office to forward 'weeklie to the burgh, 2 Edinburgh Gazettes, 2 London Gazettes and 3 Flying Posts, and 3 Postscripts with extraordinary occurrences' (Low and Low, 1889–90). Later in the century, town councils throughout Scotland can be found subscribing to the leading Edinburgh papers – the *Caledonian Mercury* and the *Edinburgh Evening Courant*. In Edinburgh, the large legal establishment almost certainly furnished a substantial number of readers. In 1780, the *Glasgow Mercury* included a letter from a 'Farmer' to the 'Noblemen, gentlemen, and farmers' of Lanarkshire regarding lowering the wages of their labouring servants (3 February 1780). The importance of readership among merchants is suggested by the relative strength of the Glasgow press, as well as the large amount of space accorded to news of shipping and maritime developments in both the Edinburgh and Glasgow papers. The *Edinburgh Weekly Journal* announced on 28 March 1798: 'We deviate somewhat from our usual mode of arrangement to give place to the following letters, received this morning, as they contain information of some importance to commercial people.'

One of the letters was from the captain of a ship sailing off the Norwegian coast. It reported that the coast was 'swarming' with French privateers who were seizing both English ships and neutral ships carrying English goods. Towards the end of the eighteenth century, the growing numbers of manufacturers associated with the cotton and linen industries appear to have increased the ranks of regular Scottish newspaper readers. In 1791, a new paper entitled the *Glasgow Courier* linked its establishment specifically with the commercial and manufacturing progress being made in 'Scotland in general, and the city of Glasgow in particular'. It further identified its potential constituency as the 'inhabitants of the Western part of Scotland' and 'those of the opulent and populous Towns on the Clyde'.

As the example of the *Glasgow Courier* indicates, the relationships between the rise of the newspaper and changing patterns of economic and social life were various and crucial. These relationships only strengthened and multiplied as the eighteenth century proceeded. The increasing size and reach of markets, the increasingly complex economic linkages between London and the provinces and between provincial cities and their urban and rural hinterlands, created the physical and social structures in which the press was able increasingly to prosper. The role of urbanization in the development of the British press would be hard to exaggerate. The town was a central actor in the creation of what has been called a national infrastructure of print in the eighteenth century. As Penelope Corfield has written, 'The growing communications industry in eighteenth-century England ... was ... a product, as well as a chronicle, of urbanization' (1982, p. 4). It was the expansion and general buoyancy of towns from the later seventeenth century that stimulated the uneven spread of printing beyond the capital. The early provincial newspapers were rarely profitable; their existence was precarious. Provincial printers survived on the printing business generated by towns and the economic activity located in them. It was only in the second half of the eighteenth century that the advertisements generated by urban businesses and services provided the basis for profitable provincial newspapers. Towns also had a strategic role to play in the expansion and improvement of communications in the eighteenth century. This reflected their marketing function. Towns constituted nodal points in commodity and product markets that were becoming national in focus. Along the roads flowed increasing volumes of goods, individuals and, more importantly in the present context, information. The expansion of the press was both a consequence and feature of this development. The growing connections between, on the one hand, different towns and, on the other, towns and rural areas were also crucial to the fortunes of the press. As the spread of coffee houses and debating clubs symbolizes, towns encouraged the readership and discussion of news print. But it was a factor of massive cultural, social and political significance that the relationship between towns and rural areas in this period was symbiotic. From the towns, news and ideas were disseminated in their surrounding areas. This took place on an impersonal and personal level. News agents conveyed newspapers, pamphlets and books to rural subscribers and purchasers. At the personal level, significant numbers of people were common visitors to the towns. The rural gentry, farmers and smaller manufacturers were all probably fairly regular visitors to their local towns. Individuals of an even more modest status also probably visited their local town periodically. Thomas Turner, the Sussex shopkeeper, was a freqent visitor to Lewes (Vaisey, 1986, *passim*). Turner was what we might call a notable in his village, East Hoathly. He was both numerate and literate. He also served a number of terms as parish overseer. Men like Turner linked town and village. They provided a conduit along which news and ideas could pass at a level well below the normally recognized elites.

The influence of markets may also have shaped and increased the demand for news in other, less visible ways. This reflected prominent aspects of economic development in this period, notably the importance of foreign trade, growing opportunities for investment in private and public stocks, and the importance of credit in the economy. All three facets of contemporary economic life were very closely affected by international politics and diplomacy. Because of this, they created powerful economic reasons for many people to attend closely to the coverage of foreign affairs and diplomacy provided by newspapers.

Investment in government debt and company stocks and bonds spread slowly from the 1690s throughout the landed and mercantile elites, especially those with close links to London (Dickson, 1967; Langford, 1989, pp. 642–3). Investment in rapidly expanding foreign trade and shipping appears to have been similarly widespread in many areas, particularly port towns. As Kathleen Wilson has written, 'port books, diaries and account books bear witness to the prosperous but otherwise quite ordinary men and women in the provinces who invested in foreign trade' (1988, p. 102; see also Brewer, 1989, p. 186). Defoe pointed to the far-reaching ramifications of domestic as well as foreign trade in the later 1720s (Defoe, 1728–9, vol. i, p. x):

> Almost all the shop-keepers and Inland Trades in sea-port towns, or even in the waterside part of London itself, are necessarily brought in to be owners of ships, and concerned at least in the vessel, if not voyage. Some of their trades, perhaps related to, or employed in the building, or fitting, or furnishing out ships ... others are concern'd in the cargoes ...

Credit networks embraced an even broader cross-section of society. Elaborate and extensive networks of credit held the eighteenth-century British economy together (see Hoppit, 1987; Earle, 1989, pp. 106–42).

The credit networks encompassed almost everyone who was economically active – merchants, shopkeepers, manufacturers, customers. One of their effects was to increase the precariousness of business. Economic progress and economic insecurity went hand-in-hand. Economic survival involved ensuring that incoming payments coincided with debt repayments as they fell due. Adverse international developments could disrupt arrangements or expectations. This is because they could easily trigger a general squeeze on public and private credit, as confidence about repayments was undermined. Julian Hoppit has studied successive financial crises in detail for the eighteenth century (Hoppit, 1987). He has shown how these crises became larger and more frequent during the second half of the eighteenth century as the economy, and thus its dependency on credit, grew. While Hoppit has also emphasized the heterogeneity of the crises, their different causes, as John Brewer has recently noted, only one 'was not in part attributable to military hostilities and the conditions of war' (1989, p. 191). The endemic nature of economic insecurity particularly among the middling ranks in society raises interesting questions about social relationships and identities. As Brewer has suggested, it may also help us explain why newspapers were so closely attended to among the mercantile and commercial classes. Newspapers offered a coverage of economic and foreign news that could not easily be matched by private sources. Merchants may have had access, in some cases, to better, more reliable and more up-to-date information, but this was necessarily very selective; their sources were usually their factors or agents in a foreign country (see esp. comments in Devine, 1975, p. 104). Where newspapers had an advantage was in conveying the general picture; they could collect news fairly rapidly from a wide variety of sources. They also appeared on a regular basis.

The precise relationship between newspapers, markets and economic activity is one that remains to be fully uncovered. Pawson has described provincial newspapers as 'instrumental in the workings of the market system, the creation of new markets, and in changing tastes and preferences' (1977, p. 33). Roger Wells has stressed the importance of the establishment of a new Monday edition of *Bell's Weekly Messenger* in 1799 to carry news of corn prices in London's Mark Lane to provincial producers, millers, factors and other wholesalers (1988, p. 24). It is, however, easy to become overly impressed by the weight of economic and commercial information carried in the pages of the press, especially in the later eighteenth century. As Richard Wilson has emphasized, there were important gaps in this information. Merchants and businessmen also had access to other sources of information, which were often private and more accurate. Wilson's remarks on this matter are worth quoting at length (1986, p. 82):

> there was an extension after 1760 of the services which the newspapers had always provided, often in incomplete fashion, for merchants and shopkeepers. These were the lists of bankrupts, prices of stock, the assize of bread, corn and malt prices (local and at Mark Lane), coal prices, shipping news and, by the late eighteenth century, London prices of meat, leather, tallow, and wines. Some newspapers gave this material in greater detail than others, and it is clear that everywhere traders and manufacturers were relying increasingly on this information .... Yet, although these services were improving ... businessmen still relied on the news and specialized information they picked up in the markets and, above all, in correspondence with their suppliers, agents, and customers. Moreover, some prices, such as sorted wool, were so complex that the newspapers could not handle them satisfactorily. And not until much later, not really until the great age of the trade journal in the second half of the nineteenth century, did businessmen obtain in printed form the detailed comment, predictions, and annual resumés of prices and trade which were essential for their calculations.

As recently noted elsewhere, the role of advertising in the eighteenth-century press is also easily exaggerated or misrepresented (Styles, 1993). Most products and services were not advertised in eighteenth-century papers. A preponderance of advertisements in English newspapers were for luxury items, rarities or property. In Scotland, advertising was even more restricted in scope. The majority of advertisements in Scottish newspapers appear to have concerned either property, private or burghal, or shipping (the advertisement of space on ships for certain journeys). In short, the relationship between the press and markets was very variable and, in many crucial areas of economic activity, virtually non-existent. For the most part, the press was dependent on, and a feature of, the development of markets, not the other way around.

CONCLUSIONS

The timing of the rise of news serials and the newspapers in Britain was linked directly to political developments. It was only during periods of intense political excitement or crisis in the seventeenth century that political control was either too weak or too disrupted to prevent the appearance of news periodicals. It is during these periods – the 1620s, the 1640s and 1650s, 1679–82 – that the potential scale of the demand for news, and the ability of printers to respond to that demand, emerges very clearly. Following the end of pre-publication censorship in 1695, the press developed very rapidly, exploiting many of the economic and social conditions for this development that were already in place by the mid-seventeenth century. These conditions became even more favourable in the eighteenth century, and the links between economic development and press strengthened and multiplied.

The changing social contours of British society were vital to the fortunes of the press. Much about the readership of eighteenth-century newspapers remains unclear. Our knowledge of the circulation of individual papers is extremely patchy. Diaries and letters provide one possible source for exploring patterns of readership, although these are often less useful than might be expected. They show that newspapers were read closely by, for example, MPs, members of the gentry, clergy, some professionals and, in the case of Thomas Turner, even modest shopkeepers. In 1740, a Wiltshire yeoman and Nonconformist school-master made the following terse entry in his diary: 'No Gazetteer'. On a number of other occasions, he recorded 'No news' (Reeves and Morrison, 1988, pp. 68–9). Politicians and newspapers often made comments about readership of papers, although these were almost always in the context of partisan debate. Many such comments emphasized (perhaps exaggerated) the popular dimensions of reader-ship, and even then were often unspecific about which groups in society they were principally referring to. The relevant division in much political rhetoric was between an ill-defined elite and the 'mob'. Such language tells us more about the continued attachment to the rule of property and its associated values at the highest political levels throughout the eighteenth century than it does about the precise social status of most newspaper readers.

What direct evidence does exist, along with much indirect evidence, suggests that the readers of eighteenth-century newspapers were a diverse group, or series of groups. One possible way of picturing eighteenth-century newspaper readers is as a series of concentric circles, with the smallest circle signifying the parliamentary classes, a larger circle their allies among the gentry, clergy and urban elites, and even yet larger circles signifying the middling sort and those on their lower boundaries, the skilled working classes. As we move out from the centre, the 'density' of newspaper reading probably diminished – proportion-ately fewer readers reading fewer newspapers. One of the larger circles, the one signifying the middling sort, was expanding in the eighteenth century. Within this circle, newspaper readership may also have become more common, particularly as relative incomes within it increased from the mid-century. It was from the growing middling ranks, both in urban and rural areas, that the biggest impetus behind the rise of the newspaper in the eighteenth century appears to have come. This model is not perfect. It was not just social status that affected access to papers, but an individual's place in social networks. Domestic servants, for example, may have had better access to newspapers than many other people of similar social standing. In 1759, the *Edinburgh Evening Courant* included a notice from a 'Footman' about a proposal for controlling access to the servant's gallery at the theatre (3 February 1759). Neither should the model be taken as implying that increasing numbers of, in Brewer's words, 'artisans, mechanics, and apprentices' did not have access to newspapers, particularly after 1760. In the 1790s, many contemporaries complained about such people reading radical papers, such as the *Sheffield Register* or *Manchester Gazette*. A 'Citizen of Glasgow' wrote to various papers in 1798 enclosing rules for the establishment of working-class reading societies, members of which would jointly purchase newspapers. He also claimed that forty-nine such clubs already existed in manufacturing districts in the west of Scotland (Smith, 1979, p. 162). If the evidence of prosecution associations is anything to go by, somewhat earlier in the century, artisans and craftsmen were reading papers not just in the larger cities and towns, such as Newcastle, Birmingham or Manchester, but also in more modest towns such as Colchester (King, 1989). Yet what the model does properly serve to underline is one of the essential facts about the early British press – that it was the capacity of the expanding middling ranks in society to get and to spend wealth that provided the foundations for, and major limitations surrounding, the growth of the press in the eighteenth century.

2 The press and politics in Britain

From the glorious revolution to the French Revolution

The perception that the press was instrumental in changing the contours and nature of the political nation in eighteenth-century Britain is a familiar one. Historians such as Geoffrey Cranfield, J.H. Plumb, John Brewer and more latterly Michael Harris have all sought to portray the press in terms primarily of change and potential challenge. It is Brewer who has gone further than any other in seeking to establish this view of the political effects of an expanding press, describing the press as a crucial component of 'an alternative structure of politics' (1976, esp. pp. 139–60). What Brewer means by this phrase is perhaps not entirely clear. At times, he seems to be suggesting that the press, or the market forces that underpinned its evolution and the wider political evolution of English society, were bringing into being a sphere of politics that rapidly threatened to submerge traditional mechanisms of political control and influence. But the term 'alternative' also encapsulates the more generalized sense of challenge that Brewer perceives the press as carrying. The press was the means by which the politically excluded, particularly among the middling ranks, were empowered. It helped them define themselves in political terms, and in opposition to the existing parliamentary classes. The terminus was support for political reform. The press was both a cause and vehicle of this new form of politics.

This perspective, of the press as a vehicle for the growing political self-definition and restiveness of the middling sort, rests on a series of assumptions about the evolution of the press itself, and about the process of politicization that it helped to bring about. It also carries with it a set of assumptions about how the prevailing system of court and parliamentary politics responded to the expanding influence of the press. But at its heart is one major assertion or perception – that as the century proceeded a conflict emerged between two political nations – a ruling oligarchy and a broader, more inclusive one – that was to prove a powerful formative influence on political identities and behaviour among significant sections of the growing middling sort in eighteenth-century Britain. Such a perception certainly helps us understand the emergence and growth of political radicalism from the 1760s, particularly in London and in certain larger cities and towns (Brewer, 1976; Money, 1977; Knox, 1979). But it simplifies and distorts the ways in which the press reacted upon politics and society. It underestimates the ways in which the press enabled the state and parliamentary classes, at crucial moments, to reinforce their hold over society. It also overlooks the extent to which oligarchical rule was always based on a series of negotiations and compromises. One of the most important insights of recent scholarship on Hanoverian Britain has been the extent to which the politics of interest was built on a delicate and extensive web of relationships binding the parliamentary classes together with wider society. The brokering of interests that held the system together conferred a measure of power on a broad range of individuals and groups (see esp. Langford, 1991; Davison, Hitchcock, Keirn and Shoemaker, 1992). The expansion and changing content of the press may have begun to alter the complex balances in these relationships. But this transformation was in most places gradual. Change was not always or even perhaps most influentially congruent with overt challenge.

The steady growth of awareness and concern about national political issues was one of the major features of political life in eighteenth-century Britain. Plotting this growth, however, has proved extremely difficult. This partly reflects its unevenness, both in terms of geography and chronology. It also reflects the fact that the mobilization of public opinion was not just a product of changes in political culture and society, but also of conjunctural factors, such as the willingness and skill with which the parliamentary classes sought to rouse opinion and external factors such as war and diplomatic hostility. There has also been a strong tendency in recent work to emphasize the liveliness and extent of popular politics even in the first half of the century. Kathleen Wilson has sought to focus attention, in this context, on the agitation surrounding Admiral Vernon in the final years of Walpolian rule (1988). Walpole's Excise Bill of 1733 provoked one of greatest outbursts of popular anger seen during the whole of the eighteenth century. Fifty-four constituencies and boroughs issued instructions to MPs calling for them to vote against the measure (Langford, 1975; Price, 1983). The anger that the measure aroused also resulted in what H.T. Dickinson has recently called 'the clearest electoral rejection of any government in the eighteenth century' (1995, p. 52) at the 1734 general election. There is also a need to remind ourselves that the capacity of some sections of provincial society to respond to national issues had also been evident since at least the seventeenth century. The party divisions of 1701–*c.* 1722, together with the frequency and extent of electoral contests under the Triennial Act, also inevitably left a layer of national political consciousness that, under the right circumstances, was easily revived throughout the early Hanoverian period and beyond.

For present purposes, however, the precise chronology of change is less important than the role of the press in increasing and deepening awareness of national political issues. As was suggested in the last chapter, the extent to which political information and news was disseminated even in the early seventeenth century should not be underestimated. News serials were only one of a number of means by which this took place. Yet the ability of newspapers to perform this function was transformed in the course of the following century. We can envisage newspapers, in this context, as not only supplementing and reinforcing existing channels of political communication – for example, between MP or notable and local elites – but also, particularly after the mid-century, carving out new channels. A good example of the former role is provided by the regular supply of newspapers that one MP, John Tucker, ensured reached his brother at Weymouth in the 1740s (Bodleian Library, MSS Don c. 101–34). These newspapers were an addition to the political information provided in correspondence between the two brothers. The link between the two men was also crucial to the dissemination of news among a network of local allies. These allies met on a regular basis in what they referred to as the 'club'. It is clear from the letters between the Tuckers that this was a forum in which national political issues were pondered and discussed.

In many circumstances, particularly in places other than large cities or towns, far from increasing the political independence of those below the elites, the early eighteenth-century press may have only reinforced their partial dependency on their social superiors for news of national political events. Some of the leading political papers sponsored by the parties of the Augustan era were aimed primarily at gentry and clergymen. This was true, for example, of Jonathan Swift's famous paper, the *Examiner* (Speck, 1972, p. 27). The pamphlets and papers sponsored by Sir Robert Walpole a few decades later were disseminated among and by prominent supporters of the ministry, as well as by Collectors of the Customs and Excises. A preponderance of names on a list of subscribers to the *Craftsman* in the mid-1730s which survives in the Cholmondeley Houghton papers are of opposition MPs. The expectation was partly that local notables would relay this information at a local level. The exclusiveness of politics was, in this way, partly retained. It was only when the circulation of London and provincial papers rose significantly, and political news and comment themselves formed a greater element in the press, that this changed significantly.

The press also did not completely or quickly undermine other forms of political communication. Many historians have tended to pass over this fact, seeing extra-parliamentary politics in this period almost exclusively in terms of the press. But other forms of disseminating news continued to have an important role to play, which reflected, in part, the continuing restrictions on press coverage of domestic politics. The numbers of manuscript newsletters grew in the early eighteenth century, until around the early 1720s. Paradoxically perhaps, the expansion of the provincial press during George II's reign actually gave them a further lease of life, since they were a better source of parliamentary news than London newspapers. Correspondence also continued to have a crucial role. In 1717, a clergyman in the northeast learnt about William Shippen's confinement in the Tower of London from a private letter (Hodgson, 1910, pp. 98–9). Some twenty years later, the Bristol MP Edward Southwell found himself being harried in the city because of the vote he had given on the famous motion of 13 February 1741 to remove Sir Robert Walpole from the King's counsels. As John Harper wrote to Southwell on 16 February (Avon County Library, Edward Southwell Papers, vol. 6):

> The Business of the House of Commons on Fryday last [13 February] Engrosses the whole discourse of this place the Hon'ble Gentlemen who divided in favour of the Great Man are much blamed amongst the number is your Hon. You are condemn'd with.[ou]t Enquiry into the Cause.

The news of this vote appears to have reached the city by private, informal means.

The importance of the press as a medium for political communication was, as alluded to above, closely shaped by political control. The reportage of parliamentary proceedings was protected before 1771 by parliamentary privilege. This privilege was reinforced and extended in 1738 (with the support of all sides of the House) and defended energetically until at least the later 1760s. The effects on the content of all newspapers, political and non-political, were far-reaching. The only undisguised information about parliamentary proceedings that London papers were able to publish was the King's speech to both houses at the beginning of a session, certain sparse details of business taken from the parliamentary *Votes*, and a list of the acts ratified by the King at the end of the session. Provincial papers were sometimes more ambitious, drawing on the accounts of manuscript newsletters such as *Dyer's Newsletter*. In this, they reflected the increasing rarity of other sources of information about Parliament the further one was from London. But even they were not immune to parliamentary correction and punishment (see Austin, 1915), and this was generally effective in restraining them.

Given the restrictions, political papers were forced to adopt and exploit a series of devices to comment obliquely on proceedings in Parliament. Essays in the leading essay papers were designed to coincide with major parliamentary debates. The arguments used in the essays were often the same as those used in debate, a fact that was sometimes far from coincidental; MPs were not above deriving their arguments from the press. Some papers, notably the influential tri-weekly evening paper the *London Evening Post*, used short verses, epigrams and cryptic remarks to comment on parliamentary events (Cranfield, 1963; R. Harris, 1993, pp. 28–31). The effects of this oblique approach to reporting have never really been systematically examined. One important effect was to make coverage of domestic politics very uneven. Geoffrey Cranfield has emphasized this in respect of the treatment of the Excise Bill of 1733 in the *London Evening Post* (1963). Cranfield described this treatment as 'curious'. This was not so much because of what was said, but because of what was left unsaid. No attempt was made to explain the Bill. The first items about it were reports of two meetings of, respectively, London merchants, traders and citizens and the capital's grocers to protest against the Bill. Subsequent issues reported the constituency instructions to MPs. On 27 January 1733, the paper 'hinted' at the content of the Bill. Its postponement was mentioned on 5 April. There was no mention of the parliamentary battles or divisions within the ministry. On 19 April reference was made to the majority of 204 on the third reading of the Bill, but this was never explained. The fragmentary, allusive style that papers were forced to adopt when commenting on Parliament must also have been an important factor limiting their impact. In London, where news of parliamentary activities and debates travelled quickly by word of mouth, through the taverns and coffee houses of Westminster and the city, such comments may have been more easily decipherable by a broad readership. Away from London, particularly where individuals lacked other sources of political intelligence, they must at times have been thoroughly bewildering. One individual wrote of an essay paper in the aftermath of the fall of Sir Robert Walpole, 'The Champion is of late so deep in his Articles of advices that we can't fathom his meaning' (Bodleian Library, MS Don c. 105, fo. 90: Richard to John Tucker, 26 April 1742).

Another source of political control, the ministry, only reinforced this tendency towards allusion and obliquity in the Augustan and early Hanoverian political press. Lord Bolingbroke's famous series of essays on history, entitled *Remarks on the History of England*, and which appeared in twenty-four successive issues of the *Craftsman* between 1730 and 1731, were partly designed to circumvent this potential threat. The same is true of the endless essays on corruption and its effects, often in the form of dream narratives or, as with Bolingbroke, historical analogies, that appeared between 1720 and 1760. An essay in the influential monthly periodical the *Gentleman's Magazine* described the current era as 'an allegorizing Age, when all real persons of ancient and modern history are exhausted' (1732, vol. 2, p. 945). Because of the extremely harsh penalties attending its expression, Jacobite argument in the early Hanoverian press was especially allusive and cryptic (for this, see Monod, 1989, pp. 15–44). It was through reducing the accessibility and immediacy of much of the political comment in the press, particularly before the 1760s, that political control had its greatest impact.

Such a conclusion appears, at first glance, to fly in the face of contemporary comments about the press, as well as recent comments on the weakness of political control of the press in this period. The ability of the ministry to police the press was certainly circumscribed after around 1720 and became increasingly so as the century proceeded. The reasons for this were partly political and partly commercial. Before the 1770s, political factors were the more important. The growing force of opposition sentiment in the City from the later 1720s made it very difficult to secure a jury that was not sympathetic to the opposition press or at least a broad interpretation of the liberty of the press (Black, 1988). The passage of an Act for Better Regulating Juries in 1729 was partly designed to overcome this difficulty (Green, 1985, pp. 322–3; but for a different interpretation, see Oldham, 1983). Under the Act, for certain specified categories of trial, the sheriffs of the City could be instructed to impanel a bench of jurors with higher property qualifications than were normally required. If the aim was to secure a more amenable jury, the results were mixed. In 1731, a guilty verdict was secured against the printer of the *Craftsman*, Richard Francklin, but at the cost of a press and public outcry. In 1744, Nicholas Paxton, the Solicitor to the Treasury and a key figure in Walpolian press policy, identified the likelihood of an unfavourable jury as a major obstacle to prosecuting press libels, a perception reiterated by the Treasury Solicitor, John Sharpe, in advice to the Duke of Newcastle in 1756 (British Library, Add. MS. 32,700, fo. 268; Add. MS. 32,687, fo. 144).

In 1752 the empanelment of a special jury did not prevent the acquittal of William Owen, printer of a pamphlet that had incurred the displeasure of the ministry and the Commons. The jury in this case also disputed the judge's instruction that it should confine itself to establishing the fact of publication rather than the libellous nature (or otherwise) of the pamphlet (Black, 1988). The arguments about the proper province of the jury in libel trials had their origins in the previous century. They rumbled on throughout the eighteenth century, only finally being resolved in favour of the jury in 1792 with the passage of Charles James Fox's Libel Act (Green, 1985).

If the behaviour of juries in libel trials was influenced by arguments about their proper province, it was also shaped by changing perceptions of the stability of Hanoverian Britain. Once the Jacobite threat was perceived by many to be diminished, a perception that grew unevenly beyond the ministry and its closest supporters from the early 1720s, the formidable powers of the ministry over the press seemed less defensible. The opposition and the press also began from around the same time to emphasize the issue of the 'liberty of the press'. This theme had obvious echoes for a political nation in which libertarian tendencies were deeply ingrained. The cry of 'English liberties' was increasingly used by all political groups, including Jacobites, to appeal for public support in the early Hanoverian period. Against this background, to mount a full-scale prosecution could easily prove counterproductive. The ministry seems to have recognized this from a relatively early stage and relied on the capacity for harassment of printers, publishers and mercuries afforded by the general warrant and the use of *ex officio* informations in libel cases (Gibbs, 1992). Such tactics were usually effective against papers that lacked political and financial support. They were markedly less success-ful against papers that had both of these, such as the *Craftsman* or *Old England, or the Constitutional Journal* in the early 1740s (Black, 1987a, pp. 164–6; R. Harris, 1993, chs 1 and 5).

The central decades of the century saw a marked decline in ministerial harassment of the press, a trend that may be partly related to the feeling among some politicians that the press was, in most cases, best left alone. The difference in attitude, in this context, between Walpole and his protégé, Henry Pelham, is marked. Even in 1741, Walpole was chasing those responsible for a pamphlet on foreign affairs which had been printed in Holland (Black, 1989b). Pelham appears to have been far more sceptical about the importance of the press (R. Harris, 1993, p. 37). As Jeremy Black has pointed out, the decline in overt political control of the press in the mid-century was to make its revival in the early 1760s politically far more controversial than it might otherwise have been

(Black, 1987a, p. 174). In 1763 the famous number 45 of John Wilkes's essay paper the *North Briton* provoked one of the then secretaries of state, Lord Halifax, to issue a general warrant for the arrest of the author, printer and publisher of the paper. With the accession of George III, the Tories were fully reconciled with the court, and landed society finally reunited. In this political context, the powers over the press possessed by the ministry were even more difficult to defend. Wilkes and allies were very adept at exploiting ambiguities or weaknesses in the law, and in using the law courts as a political platform (Brewer, 1980). Before he fled the country in early 1764, Wilkes orchestrated a series of court cases against Halifax and the officials who had implemented the warrant under which he and the printer and publisher of the *North Briton* had been taken up. In a famous series of court judgments in 1764–5, the legal power of the general warrant was destroyed. One historian has portrayed this, with justification, as an important feature in a wider liberalization of political life that took place in the early part of George III's reign (Christie, 1970, p. 18).

Most studies of the press control look at the issue from the point of view of the ministry. From this perspective, it is easy to emphasize, as I have done above, the many problems that faced the ministry in this area. But there is another side to the picture. The inconvenience of searches of premises, seizure of papers, imprisonment, payment of bail or recognizances to appear before the King's bench, appearances before the King's bench, could be great. Printers knew that the risks of political dissidence, even after 1730, were considerable. How otherwise do we explain the apparent anxiety of writers and printers about the extent of support for them from their political and financial sponsors? In 1753, James Ralph was offered the assurance that he would have the full support of the Duke of Bedford and his allies if he were prosecuted for essays published in the essay paper the *Protestor* (Carswell and Dralle, 1965, p. 218). Against this background, the level of self-censorship in the press is likely to have been greater than we imagine. Horace Walpole was astounded at the pre-emptive cuts made by the printer of the *Old England Journal* to his contributions to that paper between 1747 and 1749. As he later wrote (Lewis, 1948, vol. 13, p. 18): 'In this year (1747) and the next and in 1749 I wrote thirteen numbers in a weekly paper called Old England or the Broadbottom Journal: but being sent to the printer without a name they were published horridly deformed and spoiled.' More generally, in determining the range and pointedness of political comment in the press, political context was crucial, as was the level of political intervention in the press at any given moment. Where papers lacked close political links with parliamentary politicians, they tended to be more cautious.

They were also less well informed. It is worth pointing out that only a minority of papers had these connections at any given moment during the early Hanoverian period.

The effects of the restrictions surrounding the coverage of politics before 1760 were, then, of considerable significance. The picture that this helps to create of the early Hanoverian press, however, does need to be qualified in at least one very important respect. In seeking to understand the development of the press and its political repercussions, traditionally there has been a tendency (discernible among both political and press historians) to focus almost exclusively on the ability of the press to comment on and report domestic political episodes. The maturity of the press, its potential as an instrument of opinion, is measured against its willingness and ability to offer independent and unfettered judgement on the major issues of the day. Its other function, as a disseminator of news notably on foreign affairs, is largely over-looked. This tendency to disregard or minimize the importance of coverage of foreign affairs also reflects the fact that it is inherently a less attractive subject to historians of popular politics and the press than domestic politics and parliamentary reform. Yet it was news of foreign affairs that dominated all types of paper before 1760 (for this, see esp. Black, 1987a, pp. 197–243). It was also an aspect of affairs that, as was emphasized in the last chapter, closely affected the economic interests of a very wide range of groups and individuals – merchants, investors, bankers, speculators, tradesmen, shopkeepers. The volume of information about foreign affairs provided by the press undoubtedly fuelled a wider debate, both in London and in the provinces, about ministerial conduct of foreign policy. It is to this debate, and the practices and habits it created – lobbying and petitioning on the part of mercantile bodies, instructions to MPs protesting about the Convention of the Pardo with Spain in 1739 – that historians need to look if they want to comprehend fully how a growing press contributed to a wider awareness of national political issues before 1760.

THE LATER EIGHTEENTH CENTURY

The changes that overtook the press after 1760, both in terms of expansion and political content, are traditionally portrayed as a major factor stretching and deepening the political national during the reign of George III. Ian Christie wrote in 1970 of the press in the sixty or seventy years after 1760 producing 'a political world of depth and dimensions very different from that familiar to those who witnessed even the accession of George III' (1970, p. 20). More recently, however, Black has sought to introduce a note of scepticism to the debate (1987a, p. xiv):

> Historians discussing the press of the eighteenth century and early nineteenth century stress change and modernity and make much of the great expansion in number of copies produced in the country. However, this was often a matter of more of the same, and a reader might be forgiven for stressing continuity rather than change.

Continuities are certainly not hard to find. These are clearly apparent in respect of, for example, the circulation of individual papers, printing technology, and methods of news production and distribution. The amount of change in the provincial press *before* 1760 was very great. As Cranfield has argued, many of them had already by the accession of George III reached a state of considerable maturity (1962, esp. pp. 257–73). It was, however, among the London papers that change was most obvious after 1760. And because the provincial and Scottish press was so dependent on its London counterparts, the effects of this change were felt throughout the press.

The changes to the London press were partly a result of internal evolution and partly a result of decisive political change. The 1760s and early 1770s saw not only rapid growth in the metropolitan press but also an expansion in the space in papers devoted to the discussion of political issues. The roots of this development go back to the 1740s, with the steady advance of the letter to the press as a medium of political communication together with the steadily lessening importance of the political essay and essay paper (B. Harris, 1995c). It was, however, with the flowering in the first two decades of the new reign of tri-weekly and daily papers, such as the *Public Advertiser*, *Public Ledger*, *London Chronicle*, *London Packet* and *Morning Chronicle*, that the numbers of political letters in press took off exponentially. The implications and repercussions of this shift, both for the press and for public debate, were various. Pamphlets as well as essay papers seem to have been increasingly perceived as less effective forms of propaganda than dailies or tri-weekly papers, although much depended on purpose and intended audience. The Lord Chancellor, Lord Hardwicke, recommended in 1756 that if the ministry wanted to rebut the onslaught against it created by the loss of Minorca it should be by means of short papers placed in newspapers, since 'these short diurnal libels do more harm than large pamphlets because they spread amongst the common people' (British Library, Add MS. 32,687, fo. 146). The extent of the shift away from the pamphlet as a major form of propaganda should not be exaggerated (see Dickinson, 1990, p. 141). One estimate puts the number of separate pamphlets published on the American crisis in London in a twenty-year period from 1763 as over 1,000. Pamphlets and newspapers continued to form, as they had done in the years before 1760, a chain of communication with large numbers of pamphlets being extracted by the papers. The 1790s also saw a major extension of pamphleteering by both radical and loyalist groups. As we will see, partly because of controls on the press, the democratization of political culture that occurred in that decade almost certainly owed less to newspapers than to cheap pamphlets and other printed ephemera aimed at a popular audience and which exploited popular rhetorical strategies and styles.

In an unpublished thesis, J.P. Thomas has suggested that the ubiquity of the letter to the press in the 1760s and 1770s represented a considerable advance in the potential of the press as a vehicle for political lobbying (1982). That many contemporaries shared this perception is suggested by the concerted way in which various factions in the East India Company, colonial agents and friends of the Americans in London, and radicals such as Thomas Hollis, deluged the press with letters during these decades. Whether it also produced changes in lobbying by other mercantile groups, such as the well-organized West India merchants, is an area that requires further investigation. Keith Wrightson and David Levine have recently uncovered another use of letters to the press in an economic context during 1765. Wrightson and Levine argue that letters published, particularly in the London press but also in the Newcastle papers, materially affected the course of the 1765 Tyneside pitmen's strike. It was partly adverse publicity in the London press that convinced the mine owners to reach a compromise settlement with their workers (Wrightson and Levine, 1991, pp. 375–427). Such episodes constitute powerful evidence of the growing recognition in later eighteenth-century Britain of the importance or utility of ensuring that one's views were heard or correctly represented in the press.

Another impetus behind the massive growth in numbers of letters in the press in this period may have been a contemporaneous change in the public dimensions of parliamentary politics. From an analysis of known authorship of letters in the press at this time, Rocco Lawrence Capraro has suggested that the letters were written by, in ranking order, political writers, MPs and office holders, members of the clergy and members of the legal profession. Capraro talks of 'a new style of politics' which 'weaved itself into, but did not destroy, the fabric of existing styles of politics' (1984, pp. 306, 339). To some extent, this development was encouraged by the fragmentation, uncertainty and instability of politics in the 1760s. Between 1742 and the early 1760s, no ministry or ministers intervened on a continuous or substantial basis in the press. This reflected in part the difficulties of producing a pro-ministerial paper that could survive without substantial financial backing. In the conditions of the 1760s, with old political divisions disintegrating and new ones being constantly redrawn, there was an obvious need to establish identities and new principles of differentiation. The need to communicate on a regular basis with supporters and potential support was also greater. The looming shadow cast over the politics of the period by Pitt the Elder, who received great support from the press and particularly City opinion in the later 1750s (although this can be exaggerated), may also have acted as a stimulus. Certainly, the Earl of Bute, George III's favourite, seems to have intervened in the press because of attacks on him by Pittite supporters in the City and the press following Pitt's resignation in November 1761 (Brewer, 1973; Schweizer, 1988).

Partly on the basis of his findings about authorship in the press, Capraro has asked how far it is possible to speak about a 'dramatic' alteration in the social structure of the political press between the 1730s and 1760s. On this view, the change was more one of style than substance. Given that the authorship of many of the letters, all of which were published anonymously or under pseudonyms, is unlikely ever to be established, any judgement on this question is necessarily fairly tentative. One fact, however, that is indisputable is that the rise of the political letter was coincident with (and one cause of) a massive expansion in the volume of political comment carried in the London press. This alone was a change of substance. By creating an image of widespread political debate ostensibly open to all, irrespective of rank or connection, the proliferation of letters is likely to have further encouraged some of the broader changes in political culture evident in this period – the greater self-definition of the political nation outside London, and the development and extension of formal means for bringing the middle and lower ranks within the ambit of national politics (see pp. 47–50).

The expansion and changing nature of political comment in the press also contributed, albeit indirectly, to a change of even greater moment for the future development of the British press – the winning of the right to report on the activities of Parliament. The story of how this occurred has been told in great detail by a number of historians (Thomas, 1959, 1960; Rea, 1963, chs 11 and 12), and there is no need to repeat the story here. One element, however, that is worth drawing attention to is the motivation of many of the participants in the press. What is striking is how it was the anxiety of printers and newspaper owners to cater to public demand that caused a number of them to become involved in the challenge to parliamentary privilege. The minute books of one paper, the *St James' Chronicle*, record that the proprietors found it 'adviseable' in the later 1760s to begin publication of parliamentary proceedings (Capraro, 1984, p. 286). Wilkes's collisions with successive ministries had made politics exciting; they had increased demand for news and information about politics. The danger to cautious papers was clear: if they did not transgress the prohibition on the reporting of Parliament, they would lose readers to their less timorous counterparts. The alliance that forced Parliament to concede the right to report on parliamentary proceedings comprised, as a result, printers of both opposition and ministerial affiliation and Wilkes and his supporters in the City. It is with the Printers' Case of 1771 that Brewer's perception that an expanding market economy threatened to undermine many of the relationships and ties that restricted the public dimensions of political life in eighteenth-century England seems to be most fully borne out.

The repercussions for the press of parliamentary reporting by newspapers were enormous. While Parliament could, if it so chose, still exclude reporters from specific debates (the gallery of the House could be cleared whenever a member on the floor chose to spy 'strangers'), parliamentary reports rapidly became a staple element of the press. During sessions, accounts of the debates took up the bulk of space in most papers not devoted to advertising. In 1788 the prospectus for a new paper, the *Star*, read: 'The debates in Parliament, being subjects of universal concern, claim a respectable portion of this paper' (Black, 1991, p. 34). By opening up the views of parliamentarians and the manner in which national issues were debated in Parliament to public scrutiny, parliamentary reporting also had considerable effects on the way in which newspapers represented and commented on domestic politics. This was partly a matter of the accounts themselves furnishing material for further comment and analysis. But comment on and coverage of domestic politics also became more accessible; it became more simple and direct. The presence in papers of lengthy reports of debates must also have increased the intelligibility of many comments on political conditions and divisions by providing a context for them. Complete comprehension was not dependent, as in the first half of the century, on other sources of information or on close knowledge of parliamentary or court affairs. The press was able, in short, to reflect clearly the course of national politics in a way that political control had prevented before 1760.

One other change in the way that many London papers responded to domestic politics only reinforced the transformation in coverage of this area – an increasingly partisan standpoint. This was a general trend. Partisanship was not new to the London press in the later eighteenth century; and some papers continued either to maintain neutrality or steer clear of political controversy. But the latter were declining in number, especially from the 1780s. This trend reflected, and was part of, a wider emergence of new political divisions in national politics caused by divergent responses to Wilkes, the conflict with the American colonies and, a little later, the French Revolution. As Dror Wahrman has emphasized for the 1790s, the reporting of parliamentary debates became caught up in the trend (1992b). While reports were generally fairly accurate, the weight given to various speeches and speakers differed between different papers, as, in some cases, did the language used by some speakers.

How far were the changes evident in the London press after 1760 mirrored by changes in provincial and Scottish papers? Our knowledge of both of these elements of the later eighteenth-century press is limited. We lack a modern survey of later eighteenth-century provincial newspapers similar to that for the period before 1760 by Cranfield (but see Barker, 1994). Published work on the Scottish press is extremely patchy and, in many cases, dated (Couper, 1908; Craig, 1931; Cowan, 1946; Swinfen, 1976; Dwyer, 1989). Yet certain patterns can be identified with some confidence. The emergence and extension of parliamentary reporting in the London press only further reinforced the influence of metropolitan papers over the provincial and Scottish press. Provincial and Scottish papers devoted vast amounts of space to reports drawn from London papers. The *Edinburgh Advertiser* assured its readers in December 1782: 'During the present very important session of Parliament, the public may depend on having in this paper, a very full and impartial detail of PARLIAMENTARY DEBATES.' The *Advertiser* was in quarto format and was eight pages long. During sesssions, parliamentary reports regularly filled nearly four pages of the paper. The practice of regularly printing a letter from a London correspondent in most Scottish papers also added significantly to the volume of parliamentary news carried in these papers. This news often concerned the activities of Scottish MPs. On 28 February 1783, the *Edinburgh Advertiser*'s correspondent observed about the division that had heralded the end of Lord Shelburne's ministry:

> About thirty-six Scots members were in the House of Commons, at the division on Tuesday morning last, they were neatly divided, one half for the ministry, the other against them ... the Lord Advocate [Henry Dundas] made an able speech as usual, in favour of the administration, and had some satirical strokes on the junction of Lord North with Mr. Fox.

The printing of so much information about Parliament and parliamentary debates was one of the major ways in which the provincial and Scottish presses encouraged a greater sense of national, or in the Scottish case, British, consciousness in the eighteenth century (see also Chapter 4).

The degree to which provincial and Scottish papers became more obviously partisan in the later eighteenth century is more difficult to say, given the current state of research. The underlying trend was the same as in the London press – towards clearer partisan political identification. As was the case in the earlier part of the century, this was most obvious in large cities or towns and regions with more than one newspaper – for example, Newcastle, Norwich, Bristol, Yorkshire and the West Midlands. The trend, however, was uneven, which reflected the confusion and instability that overtook national politics in the early 1780s. Nor was every provincial paper involved. *Berrow's Worcester Journal*, for example, was maintaining a strict political impartiality as late as 1780. The pattern among Scottish papers appears to have been broadly similar. As David Swinfen has shown, during the American war, most Scottish papers were inclined to support the loyalist side (1976). In both its news coverage and comment, the *Glasgow Mercury* was clearly supportive of Lord North and the war as late as 1780. Its political leanings were especially evident in the selections it made from American newspapers. On 9 November 1780 the paper reprinted a series of items from the loyalist *New York Royal Gazette*, including an address to the Congress complaining about the fiscal impositions laid by the former. The same paper criticized the English Association movement, seeking to raise the spectre of the civil wars of the previous century. During 1782–3, the *Edinburgh Advertiser* showed consistent support for the Shelburne ministry and the rising star of that ministry, William Pitt the Younger. This reflected in large part the identification of Pitt with prospects for moderate parliamentary reform. In 1790, such was the general sympathy for the French Revolution displayed in the Scottish press that pro-ministerial supporters in Scotland established the *Edinburgh Herald* to supply the need for, as one of them put it, a 'truly constitutional paper' (Meikle, 1912, p. 44).

Political control and intervention appears to have had little influence on the trend towards greater partisanship disclosed throughout the press in the later eighteenth century – that is, until the 1790s. Ministerial and opposition subventions to the press were either intermittent or small-scale before the 1790s. The combination of war with France (after 1793) and anxiety about the activities of radicals created a degree of alarm about the effects of the press that had last been witnessed in

England in the 1710s regarding a popular Jacobite press (for the latter see Chapman, 1983; Hyland, 1986). In late 1792 and again in 1799 schemes were proposed and discussed to introduce tighter statutory regulation of the press, but these were never taken up (Mori, 1992, p. 80; Black, 1994b, pp. 59–61). In 1789 legislation was passed outlawing the hiring of papers from hawkers, and the stamp tax was increased in 1789 and 1797, in all cases as policing measures. In 1798 further legislation compelled the recording of the names and addresses of printers and publishers on every copy of a paper, as well as forbidding the export of papers to enemy countries. In 1799 a register of printing presses was introduced. Apart from these measures, the government relied on the use of *ex officio* informations and local initiative to police the radical press.

The effect of the various forms of political control utilized was, broadly speaking, to undermine, although not completely eliminate, a radical presence in the periodical press (Schweizer and Klein, 1989; Black, 1987a, pp. 185–8; Smith, 1979, esp. chs 5 and 6). The radical London paper the *Argus* was destroyed as a result of ministerial action in 1792. Radical publishers of various provincial papers found themselves subject to hostility from the local bench and local loyal mobs. The *Leicester Chronicle* and *Manchester Herald* were both brought to an end in 1793, and the *Sheffield Register* in the following year. The editor of another Sheffield paper, the *Sheffield Iris*, was imprisoned in 1795 and 1796, which eventually moderated the paper's political edge. In Scotland, the Edinburgh radical paper the *Gazetteer* was suppressed after the third Scottish Convention of British radicals in 1793. The *Glasgow Advertiser* also faced a sedition charge in 1793. Some London papers that had initially espoused radical views in the early 1790s became more cautious after 1793. How far radical and reformist sentiment continued to find an outlet in both the Scottish and provincial presses throughout the 1790s is a subject that needs further investigation. H.T. Dickinson has recently emphasized the predominance of loyalist sentiment in the English provincial press in the 1790s (Dickinson, 1990; 1995, p. 272). But there do appear to have been some papers that continued to follow a radical or moderate reformist line through the decade. Black has recently pointed to the discussion of radical views in two provincial papers – the *Cambridge Intelligencer* and the *Bury and Norwich Post*. Another paper that continued to promote radical principles was the *Manchester Gazette*. In 1792, the *Derby Mercury* was following a broadly reformist line. The *Glasgow Advertiser* in Scotland maintained a similar stance despite the hostile legal action in 1793. The *Preston Review and*

County Advertiser declared in late June of 1793 'A Faithful Historian is of no country; and the conductor of an impartial Newspaper is of no party' (29 June 1793). In keeping with this non-partisan stand, the paper included a generally commendatory biographical sketch of the leading Whig and reformer Sir Charles Grey in its issue of 23 September 1793. It also, however, consistently opposed popular radicalism. Among the London press, a number of papers followed an opposition and/or reformist line from the early 1790s. A report about the circulation of papers among radicals in Tiverton in the later 1790s lists four London papers – *Bell's Messenger*, the *Weekly Observer*, the *Recorder* and the *General Evening Post* – as among the 'Jacobins' papers read chiefly here about' (O'Gorman, 1989, pp. 286–7). James Perry's *Morning Chronicle* and Daniel Stuart's *Morning Post* both maintained pro-opposition lines. There are even some examples of ministerial papers publishing pro-opposition items (Schweizer and Klein, 1989). For the later part of the decade, John Cookson has argued that it was only in a moment of extreme reaction on the part of the ministry in 1798 that liberal reformers were unable to find a voice in the press. Otherwise, he suggests, the picture of their presence in the press is of surprising resilience (Cookson, 1982, ch. 4). As emphasized earlier, Jacobin radicals were for the most part, however, forced into using what Wells has dubbed 'the subterranean press' – handbills, pamphlets, posters, political songs, parodies and cartoons – to promulgate their message. Wells has recently described the production of these forms of propaganda as 'a growth industry after 1795'. It was also an industry that, unlike the periodical press, the government and its local supporters found very difficult to police (Wells, 1988, p. 144).

Apart from acting to police the content of the press, the ministry in the 1790s also intervened directly in the press. As Aspinall emphasized over half a century ago, the level of subsidization, either direct or indirect (through the placement of official notices and advertisements), reached levels last seen under Walpole in the 1730s (Aspinall, 1949, p. 68). Of fourteen daily papers in existence in 1790, the Treasury provided subventions to nine. Two loyal papers were established with government help at the end of 1792 – the *Star* and the *True Briton*. In Scotland, the 1790s saw official subsidization of a paper, the *Edinburgh Herald*, for the first time (Cowan, 1946, preface). The impact of this intervention, especially among the London press, however, can be questioned. As Karl Schweizer and Rebecca Klein have recently underlined, by this period, the financial security and well-being of most papers was sufficient for the withdrawal of subsidies not to matter a great deal.

The level of the subsidies was also generally quite low. Schweizer and Klein have concluded that the only 'steadfast' adherents of the ministry in this period were John Walter of the *Times* and Henry Sampson Woodfall of the *Public Advertiser*. Woodfall retired in 1793, and other papers proved 'disappointing to the ministry'. Another factor was also working against ministerial influence – a wider trend among all London papers, both opposition and ministerial, towards higher standards of reporting and more impartial reporting (Schweizer and Klein, 1989). The French Revolution played a significant part in this, first by stimulating the demand for news of the revolution, and second because, through its proximity, it encouraged papers to experiment with new ways of gathering more immediate and up-to-date information, including direct reporting. James Perry, joint owner–editor of the *Morning Chronicle*, for example, was sent to Paris to report on events in 1791 (Christie, 1970, p. 344).

Most elements of the press of the later eighteenth century, then, showed important changes in content from the press of the period before 1760, changes that considerably enhanced the role of the press in encouraging greater awareness of national politics. But how did this press react on different groups in society? How far did the press act as an agent of politicization?

Such questions are very hard to answer with any degree of certainty. The gaps in our knowledge are too numerous. We are only able to specify in broad terms those groups from which newspaper readers are most likely to have come. Why people read newspapers is as difficult to be precise about as it is today. Eighteenth-century newspapers sought to offer variety and entertainment as well as news. Readers were drawn to politics for different reasons, many of them having little to do with politics – instruction, entertainment, a need for commercial information and news about shipping. Many historians tend to assume that interest in politics was 'natural'. This is a dangerous and ill-founded assumption. Politics was interesting to many groups for different reasons, but it was also ignored by many groups for similarly diverse reasons. Even if we assume, as the evidence of the newspaper press itself suggests, that many of the readers of newspapers attended closely to news and comment about national politics, what effect this had on their perceptions is impossible to say. Contemporary comments about the press were usually made in the context of hostile remarks about popular opinion. An irresponsible press is used to explain popular hostility on a particular issue. A more sceptical reading, however, might suggest that, particularly as papers became more obviously partisan, they were read by many individuals who broadly shared the same political views. The circumstances in which newspapers were read are obviously relevant here. Some coffee houses carried an extensive selection of newspapers of different political principles. As a visitor to Glasgow in 1792 commented (quoted in Meikle, 1912, p. 43n.):

> The great subscription coffee-room is supported by certain annual contributions of more than six hundred of the principal citizens of Glasgow and members of the university. Half of the newspapers of London, the Gazettes from Ireland, Holland, and France, and a number of provincial journals and chronicles of Scotland and England, besides reviews, magazines, and other periodicals, are objects of subscription.

Readers in this and similar institutions probably read a wide range of newspapers. The context for much newspaper readership, however, was more partisan. The Leicester Arms, or Freeth's Coffee House as it was known, in Birmingham, for example, recently described by John Money, was a haunt of Birmingham reformers and radicals (Money, 1977, pp. 103–4, 108–9). In Tiverton in Devon in the 1790s certain weekly papers were collected at the Phoenix Inn Tavern and Coffee House 'where there are several Clubs till the next morning' (O'Gorman, 1990, pp. 286–7). The increasingly clear identification from the 1780s of many papers with parliamentary parties or factions probably acted as a major limitation on their circulation. Perry's *Morning Chronicle* almost certainly gained most of its readership from Whig or opposition supporters.

The press, however, had a more creative role to play than this suggests. It was a major force behind the increasingly public nature of much politics. It was also the principal vehicle for changing forms of extra-parliamentary politics. These developments were closely interlinked. The potential of the press as, in Michael Harris's phrase, a 'circuit of political communication' between locality and centre had been sporadically exploited in the early Hanoverian period (M. Harris, 1984). The crucial episodes were campaigns of instructing MPs which took place in 1733, 1739–42, 1753 and 1756. In these campaigns, the press acted as instructor and publicizer. Usually, the starting point was an instruction issued by the City of London to its four MPs. This was widely reprinted in the opposition press, and calls were made for other boroughs and constituencies to follow suit. The instructions that were forthcoming were all prominently printed in the press. The role of the press in these campaigns can be exaggerated. Behind at least some of the instructions, it was the encouragement of MPs that was crucial. Whether the sentiments they expressed were genuinely or widely felt in particular localities is debateable. But the momentum that gathered behind such campaigns cannot be dissociated from the publicity given to them in the press. In the second half of the eighteenth century, the petition emerged as the major instrument of extra-parliamentary politics (see esp. Dickinson, 1990, pp. 142–3). As was the case before 1760, papers gave these expressions of local and national opinion considerable prominence. It was, however, the ways in which provincial papers were used to support these demonstrations of opinion that showed the most obvious changes.

This was yet another aspect of their increasingly partisan and overtly political nature after 1760. It also reflected the increasingly sophisticated way in which traditional bodies – for example, town councils, county meetings, grand juries, as well as other local groups – and individuals sought to exploit provincial papers. The best-known example of this is Christopher Wyvill, architect of the Association movement of 1779–85. The care that Wyvill took in planting information and comment in the York and Leeds papers has been documented by Christie (1970, pp. 279–81; see also Barker, 1994). Meetings were advertised well in advance; items were written and published to prepare opinion in advance of meetings; the resolutions of meetings were subsequently advertised in a wide range of London and local papers. The use of the press made by Wyvill and the Association movement appears to have encouraged other extra-parliamentary groups to exploit the press more fully in the 1780s. This was true of campaigners against the slave trade in 1788 and 1792, and Dissenters in 1787, 1788 and 1790. Opponents of some of these groups adopted similar methods. In 1790, the SPCK and various figures in the Church of England, notably Bishop Samuel Horsley, encouraged a nationwide campaign of public meetings to protest against any attempt to repeal the Test Acts. As F.C. Mather has recently argued, this movement developed largely spontaneously in reaction to the meetings held by various Nonconformists (1992, pp. 71–81). The first to respond were the Leeds clergy. The news of this meeting was transmitted throughout the country by printing the notices and resolutions of the meeting in newspapers. A meeting called for the same purpose in Warwickshire decided to send its resolutions to the London, Birmingham and other provincial papers. Richard Wilson has recently shown how certain commercial groups also increasingly used the press in similar ways (1986). This aspect of the press is something about which we currently know too little. Wilson has examined the use of the press by Yorkshire worsted and woollen merchants, but the press also played a role in the opposition of a diverse body of manufacturers to Pitt's fiscal policies and initiatives with respect to trade with Ireland in the mid-1780s, as well as the successful opposition to the fustian and shop taxes of 1785. The Scottish press was exploited in a series of agitations in favour

of a Scottish militia bill in 1759–60 and 1782, and burgh and parliamentary reform in 1782–3. The press was also used by various parishes and
bodies in the struggles over patronage in the Church of Scotland. In
February 1783, the nine Incorporated Trades of Dundee decided to
publish resolutions on burgh reform and church patronage in 'the
Edinburgh, Glasgow, and Aberdeen papers' (*Edinburgh Advertiser*, 28
February 1783).

The anxiety of increasing numbers of extra-parliamentary bodies to
publicize their activities in the press (see also Innes, 1990, for the use of
the press by individuals and bodies seeking social reform) reflected a
recognition not just of the contribution that the press could make to
mobilization at a local level. It also reflected an awareness of the
importance of emulation as a force for stimulating extra-parliamentary
activity. The publicity given to particular initiatives helped to spur
similar initiatives elsewhere. It transformed the context in which
individuals and groups in particular localities operated. It reinforced
the sense of inclusion in a greater movement. The *Freeman's Magazine*,
the voice of the Newcastle radicals in the early 1770s, recorded that 'they
published in the London newspapers, to inform their friends and
brethren of their fears, concerning the public interest' (*The Freeman's
Magazine: or, the Constitutional Repository*, Newcastle, 1774, p. vi). The
elaborate efforts that, as Brewer has shown, the Wilkite radicals made to
mount local celebrations and processions at various key moments, for
example on Wilkes's release from prison in 1770 (see esp. 1983), are
perhaps only fully intelligible in a similar context. The press gave them a
national as well as local dimension. Their purpose was expressive as
much as instrumental. They were designed to show, not least to fellow
radicals, the extent of support for Wilkes throughout the country. In
1745, 1792–3, 1794 and 1797–8 loyalist demonstrations had similar
intent and effect. In 1798, for example, the *Edinburgh Weekly Journal*
carried a number of paragraphs about the progress of the voluntary
contribution. On 7 February 1798, the paper observed:

> Our Readers will participate in our Satisfaction, in announcing the
> rapid progress of the Voluntary Contribution towards the exigencies
> of the state. At a late hour on Wednesday last, we were enabled to
> mention the noble example shewn by the Corporation of this City, in
> subscribing TWO THOUSAND POUNDS for the service of their
> country, to which we were soon after enabled to add, that the
> gentleman who worthily fills the office of chief magistrate of the city,
> had subscribed for himself *TWO HUNDRED POUNDS*.

During the '45, many of the reports of local loyal activity are to be found in the majority of London and provincial papers (B. Harris, 1995a, 1995b). Some of the paragraphs describing loyal activities and initially printed in local papers were clearly drawn up with a national audience in mind. These reports show how, partly through the press, a sense of local pride was being defined in terms of contribution to a national cause.

The relationship between the press and politicization was, therefore, complex and multifaceted. How we should interpret this feature of the development of the press in terms of the political identity and habits of the growing numbers of the middling ranks is examined in Chapter 4. A point, however, that is worth stressing in the present context is that it is, as should be clear by now, a simplification to think of the development of extra-parliamentary politics in the eighteenth century solely or primarily in terms of radicalism and 'popular' political activity (for this, see esp. Black, 1993b). Much extra-parliamentary activity tended in the opposite direction – for example, the outcry over the Jew Bill in 1753, the loyalist movements of 1745–6 and the 1790s. Much radicalism was also as much conservative in inspiration as progressive (see esp. Christie, 1962; Langford, 1991, esp. pp. 466–7). This was as true of the Wilkite movement as of the Association movement. Many of the supporters of Wilkes were motivated by a perceived threat to long-established English liberties such as the right of election of MPs (Langford, 1989, pp. 377, 380). The contradictions in the Association movement among the country gentry and freeholders and the advanced, more speculative radicalism of certain metropolitan supporters of the movement rapidly undermined the momentum that it acquired in late 1779 (Christie, 1962). Much extra-parliamentary activity was also designed less to challenge the system than work within it. The sections of society involved were only in a weak sense excluded. This, for example, is true of the 38,000 freeholders who signed petitions on economical reform in 1780, or the gentry and clergy who met to draw up instructions to MPs on the Jew Bill. The re-emergence of party, or at least of stronger national political divisions, after the late 1760s reinforced this trend. Party became a growing focus for the expression of political sentiments within the system (Phillips, 1982). Black has recently spoken of the need to 'stress the diversity and complexity of public opinion' as well as the diversity of the press itself (Black, 1993b, p. 70). The sum of the changes to the press may have made political reform more likely in the long run. It did not, however, make it inevitable.

CONCLUSIONS

The changes in the political role of the press during the eighteenth century were far-reaching. The press provided an increasingly national forum for the expression of political views. In this way, it reinforced the strength and purchase of a national political culture. The influence of London and the London press was crucial to this process. Through its press, London provided the national focus for the expression of views and transmission of information.

An important aspect of the growing national focus of political culture in the later eighteenth century was the reporting of parliamentary debates and divisions. As historians are increasingly showing, the eighteenth-century Parliament, through its legislative functions as well as its role as a forum for political discussion, was a force for political integration (see esp. Langford, 1991; Innes, 1990; Davison *et al.*, 1992). By providing a focus for the debate of various aspects of economic and social policy, the press accentuated this role. The reporting of debates in Parliament also served to open up politics in new ways; it was a major element in the increasingly public nature of eighteenth-century politics. In 1738 the MP William Pulteney, then in opposition and actually courting popular support, suggested that to allow press reporting of parliamentary proceedings 'looks very much like making them [MPs] accountable without doors for what they say' (Cobbett, 1806–20, vol. 10, pp. 800–12). In 1797 William Windham, who had joined the ministry of Pitt the Younger in 1794, complained, against the background of the naval mutinies at Spithead and La Nore, that the press threatened to 'essentially change the relations of the People with the Commons' (quoted in Black, 1993b, p. 75). MPs of the later eighteenth century were only too aware that their speeches were public statements in a way that those of most MPs of the early Hanoverian period were not. Some MPs, because of this, prepared versions of their speeches for publication. The effects of greater publicity were reinforced by the growth of new political divisions among many sections of society. Many MPs found themselves forced to declare their principles in a very public manner to their existing or potential constituents. Provincial papers magnified the effects of these utterances. The press reflected and encouraged, in short, a much sharper awareness of national issues. It helped to provide much of political life with a common language, a language derived from parliamentary politics and debate.

By linking locality and centre increasingly effectively, the press also, finally, began to change the nature of public politics in other ways. In this process, there was a mixture of the old and the new. The press reacted on and subtly altered established means of expressing political opinion – most obviously, the grand jury address, county meeting or demonstration. It also encouraged the development of additional means of political agitation, such as the petition, and closer, more formal linkages between different elements of a political campaign. In these ways, the press helped to stretch the social and geographical boundaries of the political nation, as well as to change its nature. These changes did not necessarily or directly threaten traditional forms of politics. Nor did they quickly undermine them. One of the reasons for this was that the political system and traditional political relationships were also developing and changing at the same time.

3   The press in eighteenth-century France

The history of the French press begins in 1631 when, under the direction of Cardinal Richelieu, Théophraste Renaudot founded the *Gazette de France* (Solomon, 1972). The Frondes in the 1650s saw a number of short-lived journals (a recent estimate is forty-seven between 1648 and 1657), and the publication of somewhere in the region of 5,000 pamphlet-type publications – the Mazarinades (Sgard, 1991, vol. ii, pp. 1131–40). But the real development of the French press commences in the 1680s, with the expulsion of the Huguenots from France. This provided the impetus behind the establishment of a lively, cosmopolitan French-language press on France's borders (see Eisenstein, 1992). In so far as old-regime France had a genuine information and political press, it was owing to these papers.

Despite, or perhaps rather because of this, in recent years a growing number of French historians have begun to argue that the press had a much more important and creative role under the old regime than traditional accounts of the period have allowed (see the summary of recent debate in Censer and Popkin, 1987). These historians argue that the press played a vital role in the transformation of political culture in pre-revolutionary France. The press helped to construct and define a politics of contestation, a politics that altered notions of political legitimacy in France (Baker, 1987, 1989). Public opinion was increasingly invoked, albeit in a largely rhetorical sense, as the arbiter in political disputes. It was this politics that Jacques Necker sought unsuccessfully to exploit as he attempted to rescue the country from its acute financial plight in the late 1780s. The publication of his *Compte Rendu au Roi* in February 1781 was a striking witness to the new forms of politics that had been developing in the previous thirty years or so.

In this chapter, we will be looking more closely at the French press before 1789 to identify any similarities and to isolate more clearly the many contrasts both with its British counterpart and the revolutionary press in France. One implication of much recent work on the pre-revolutionary French press is that the comparisons with Britain and the revolutionary period are often drawn too crudely. Both propositions deserve careful examination. The bulk of this chapter will investigate the first of these – the comparison with the British press. In the penultimate section, we will go on to look at how the French press was transformed by the French Revolution, and the contribution that it made, in its changed guises, to revolutionary politics.

Comparative history has many pitfalls. There is always a danger of the comparisons being superficial. This is a particular risk in respect of the press. Perhaps the dominant image of the press in all periods since the invention of printing has been of a neutral technology, a technology that erodes or ignores political boundaries, that possesses inherent political dynamics. This image is not necessarily entirely ill-founded. Yet it is important not to lose sight of the role of political, economic and social factors in mediating the influence of the press. Different levels of literacy, urbanization and commercialization, differing social relations and structures, and very different political contexts, all inevitably played a significant part in shaping some of the contrasts between the press in France and Britain. The importance of some of these factors should become apparent in the course of this chapter.

There is also another difficulty that is worth drawing attention to at this stage. This is that in certain cases there appears to be some confusion or ambiguity about what is being compared. There is a tendency among French historians not to differentiate clearly between different forms of periodical publication. Papers that were designed primarily to carry news are often spoken about in the same context as the growing number of specialist papers devoted to cultural and scientific topics. This reflects at least two factors. First, in typographic terms the newspaper in France had yet to become very distinctive. In appearance, they are difficult to distinguish from other periodicals, and even from pamphlets and books (Eisenstein, 1992, p. 8). Second, and perhaps more importantly, it reflects the historiographical background. Following the pioneering work of Daniel Mornet (1967), studies of the French or French-language press have often been designed as contributions to a wider debate about the cultural origins of revolutionary politics. In this context, it has been their role as disseminators of the enlightenment that has been seen as important. Jacques Godechot (Bellanger *et al.*, 1969), and more recently Roger Chartier (1991), J.R. Censer (1994) and Elizabeth Eisenstein (1992) have all placed the role of the press in this context. Here the influence of Jürgen Habermas is clearly discernible. Habermas saw the emergence of a new political space, 'the public sphere', as one of the defining features of eighteenth-century political, cultural and social development. The nature of this space as conceptualized by Habermas has already been discussed at an earlier stage in this book. The important point to emphasize here is that he saw the development of a critical literary and cultural public as a precondition or precursor of the emergence of public opinion in politics. One effect of Habermas's influence on French historiography has been to reinforce the tendency to see the press in eighteenth-century France as but one dimension of a wider culture of print.

There is, then, a need to be unambiguous at the outset about what is being compared. The principal focus of this chapter will be newspapers, as it is throughout this book, in other words periodical publications that included substantial regular comment on, and/or coverage of, foreign and domestic events. As we have seen, such a definition has obvious limitations. It focuses on one aspect of press content to the exclusion of the massive volume of literary, cultural, moral and social comment carried in both the British and French press in the eighteenth century. Yet the reason for thus confining our field of enquiry is that it gives any investigation a clear focus. It is also arguable that in so far as we are interested in convergences and divergences between political cultures in the two countries, it is the dissemination of news and comment on politics that is most important. This perception has not been lost on historians of the French revolutionary press. Pierre Rétat, for example, has argued that one of the ways in which the revolutionary press transformed political culture was by fundamentally altering perceptions of events (1985; Labrosse and Rétat, 1989). The daily reports of events which the revolutionary press created gave readers, Rétat argues, a new experience of living through an unfolding narrative which commenced with the storming of the Bastille on 14 July 1789. The press created, in other words, a continuous political narrative, a narrative that individuals in very different places and contexts could feel themselves part of. In this way, the press appeared to hold out the prospect of creating a new collectivity of politically aware citizens. To what extent such a press existed under the old regime in France, if at all, is one of the issues that we will need to clarify.

Any assessment of the circulation and readership of the press in eighteenth-century France is hampered by a lack of statistics. Very few account books survive, particularly for political or information papers. Many of the other figures that we possess are one-off estimates made by the papers themselves and on that basis are suspect. Unlike in Britain, there are also no relevant taxation records. Whatever figures we come up with are in the nature of rough guides to the sorts of magnitudes involved. As in the case of Britain, estimates of circulation do not, moreover, neatly correspond with readership. Each copy was likely to have been read by a number of readers, although, as we will see, we actually know rather little about the circumstances in which most newspapers were read in France in this period.

The growing body of bibliographical work on the eighteenth-century French press makes building up a picture of growth in the French press in the eighteenth century much less difficult than it would have been a few years ago. Ignoring for the time being the different sorts of periodicals, as far as papers published in France and French-language periodicals circulated in France are concerned, the pattern is one of steadily strengthening growth from around 1730 (Sgard, 1984). Between 1720 and 1729, forty new titles were founded. Two decades later (1740–9), the figure was ninety. Between 1770 and 1779 it reached 148, and in the last decade of the *ancien régime* 167. As Jean Sgard has shown, as the century proceeded, the numbers of new periodicals surviving for a considerable length of time also increased – another indication that the market for periodical publications was strengthening. A crucial year in the history of the French press was 1759. It was in this year that the Paris publishers of the *Affiches de France* began to market the right to create provincial editions. Before that date, government policy had restricted the growth of provincial papers, although provincial editions of the official *Gazette de France* had been published in the first half of the century. As Gilles Feyel has written, the early years of the *affiches* were characterized by slowness and timidity (1984). Between 1759 and 1770 only nine provincial papers emerged that remained in existence for any time. After this, however, the rate of growth markedly increased. The period 1772–7 saw ten papers come into existence, and twenty papers between 1779 and 1788. By 1788, there were forty-four provincial *affiches* being published throughout most of the country.

How many of these papers, however, fall within our designated area of enquiry (papers that regularly carried news of or comment on political affairs)? And in what sorts of numbers did they circulate? It has to be stressed here that the data are very patchy. As a number of French historians have shown, there are also enormous problems when it comes to categorizing eighteenth-century periodicals. Sgard has proposed a binary division between political gazettes and literary journals, but in practice this distinction tends to break down in the face of the miscellaneous content of many papers. Nevertheless, drawing on the bibliographical data collected by contributors to the *Dictionnaire de journaux, 1600–1789* (Sgard, 1991), an outline can be built up. Like the French press as a whole, the Parisian press was tightly controlled. This restricted very closely the number of Paris-based papers that strayed into political affairs. At any time during the century, the number of papers published in Paris that carried political news and information never exceeded four or five. (This figure includes the clandestine Jansenist journal, the *Nouvelles ecclésiastiques*.) Until 1778, the official paper of record, the *Gazette de France*, held a nationwide monopoly on political news. In that year the monopoly was taken away from the *Gazette* and bought by Charles Joseph Pankcoucke, the nearest eighteenth-century France had to a press baron. Pankcoucke produced a political supplement, the *Journal de Bruxelles*, to go with his *Mercure de France*. He was also responsible for the *Journal de Genève* from 1774 and the *Gazette* from 1786. The political sections of the *Journal de Bruxelles* and the *Journal de Genève* were identical from 1778. Both the *Journal de Bruxelles* and *Journal de Genève* purported to be published outside France, but were in fact produced inside the country. Two other Paris-based papers that were allowed to print political news prior to 1789 were the *Journal de Paris*, which appeared daily from 1777, and the *Journal général de France*, a tri-weekly paper that was founded in 1784. The provincial *affiches* appear to have avoided infringing on the monopoly of political news enjoyed by, first, the *Gazette*, and then Pankcoucke. As Jeremy Popkin has recently commented of the *Journal du Hainault et du Cambrésis*, which he suggests was typical of the provincial papers published at the end of the old regime (1993a, p. 438), 'Until revolutionary politics elbowed its way into the paper's columns, the content included verse, book reviews, articles on medicine and science, and a regular series on local history.' Even during the pre-revolutionary crisis of 1787–8, only a few provincial papers provided substantial information about political events (Albertan and Albertan, 1989). Some even remained silent in 1789 (Gough, 1988, p. 27).

As already emphasized, the most important vehicles for political news and comment in eighteenth-century France were French-language papers published outside France, particularly, but not exclusively, in the Low Countries and Holland. The most famous of these were the foreign gazettes, among which the *Gazette de Leyde* stands out in terms of sustained influence and importance (Popkin, 1989; Duranton, Labrosse and Rétat, 1992). The numbers of foreign gazettes allowed to circulate in France increased as the century progressed. Before the 1750s, only five were allowed to enter the country, although at a price that severely circumscribed their circulation. The inflated cost of these papers encouraged pirate editions to be published in a number of towns (Censer, 1994, p. 162). In 1759 there was a change in official policy and the borders were opened to foreign papers, and the cost of subscription, now organized through an official bureau based in Paris, was reduced by around 400 per cent (from 120 livres to 36). By the 1770s and 1780s the number of gazettes regularly circulating in France had climbed to around nine. As well as the gazettes, there were also a number of more polemical papers published in London from the 1770s and allowed to enter the country with official connivance. The most famous and widely circulated of these was Simon-Nicolas-Henri Linguet's *Annales politiques, civiles et littéraires* (Popkin, 1987, 1988). Linguet's paper was highly idiosyncratic in tone and content. Discussion of politics was conducted at an abstract level. As Censer has recently written, Linguet 'rarely commented on particular policies or developments' (Censer, 1994, p. 50). Two papers that commenced life in London in the 1770s and which did provide news and comment on current affairs and politics were the *Affaires de l'Angleterre et de l'Amérique* (1776–9) and the more important *Courrier de l'Europe* (1776–92). Following action by the British ministry, the latter was published in Boulogne from 1778.

As in Britain, a major factor influencing the circulation of newspapers in France was war and international tension. The Seven Years War (1756–63) was a period of rapid progress for all journals of information. The boost that the war gave to the circulation of the *Gazette de France* has been documented by Feyel (1982, 1988). Patchy evidence only allows us to see the development in outline. In 1749, between 6,800 and 8,800 copies of the *Gazette* were being distributed throughout France. Around 20 per cent of these were for the Parisian market. In 1758, the provincial edition of the paper reached 12,000 copies. Feyel has suggested a probable total print run of around 15,000. After the Seven Years War, the circulation of the *Gazette* fell appreciably. The difficulties that the paper found itself in were owing partly to competition from the foreign gazettes but also to the burgeoning clandestine pamphlet press in Paris, the so-called *libelles*. Various attempts were made to revive the paper between the 1760s and 1780s, but it was the American War that provided the much-needed boost to circulation. In 1781, its circulation appears to have climbed back up towards its previous peak, reaching around 12,000. By the mid-1780s, however, this had fallen back to around 7,000.

The evidence for an increase in circulation throughout the political press during the American War is fuller than for any of the earlier eighteenth-century wars. Pankcoucke's *Mercure de France* had a maximum circulation of 20,000 in 1784, although it quickly dropped back after the end of war, to around 11,000. The peak circulation of any one of the foreign gazettes in France was probably between 2,000 and 4,000. The *Courrier d'Avignon*, published, as the title indicates, in the papal enclave of Avignon, had a circulation in France of 4,000 in 1778

(Moulinas, 1974, pp. 351–2). During the same period, around 2,500 copies of the *Gazette de Leyde* were being sold in France. The *Courrier de l'Europe* had a circulation of around 6,000 in 1784, although, again like other papers, this dropped back significantly in the following few years. Figures for Linguet's *Annales* are much harder to come by, not least because of the existence of a number of pirate editions. Modern estimates range from 10,000 to 20,000 (Sgard, 1991, vol. i, p. 1140; Popkin, 1988).

What sorts of overall figures for press circulation in France at the end of the American War do the above print runs suggest? Any figure that we come up with is necessarily in the nature of an educated guess; the gaps in information remain significant. Nevertheless, a rough calculation suggests that the absolute upper limit of the weekly circulation of papers in France carrying news of and comment on political events around 1783–4 was somewhere in the region of between 80,000 and 90,000. This, it has to be stressed, is a very generous estimate and refers to the period in which interest in the press was at its height. Feyel has estimated an overall circulation in the same period of over 60,000, although this does not include Linguet's *Annales* (1992, p. 96). Censer has put forward a figure that includes Linguet's paper of over 80,000 (1994, pp. 11–12). The figure at other times was almost certainly considerably lower. As Popkin has noted, usual sales of foreign gazettes were probably of the order of a few hundred per copy (1987, p. 86). Nevertheless, during the central decades of the century the general trend was undoubtedly strongly upwards. Censer has recently estimated overall circulation in the 1740s at around 15,000 (1994, p. 12).

By themselves, these figures do no more than suggest, as with the figures on new titles cited earlier, that the market for papers was growing substantially from around the later 1730s. To put them into their proper context, they need to be seen against the background of a growing population and increasingly wealthy and numerous middling class. The French population grew by about 7.1 million in the eighteenth century, that is about twice the increase in Britain (3.6 million) (these and other figures cited below come from Jones, 1991). The bourgeoisie, or middling stratum of French society, grew at a much faster rate, by a factor of about three. (Bourgeoisie is here defined as persons who were non-noble, comfortably off and mostly living in towns.) One estimate for the size of the bourgeoisie which has gained acceptance from a number of historians is 2.3 million. The historian whose figure this is also suggests that the same group only numbered between 700,000 and 800,000 in 1700. The French nobility in 1789 numbered somewhere around 120,000. French society was also becoming more urbanized. Between 1725 and 1789, the urban population rose by over 40 per cent. In 1789, France's urban population numbered around 5.3 million. The English figure was 2.3 million. The rate of growth of the political or information press, therefore, comfortably exceeded the rate of growth of population and almost certainly exceeded the rate of growth of the bourgeoisie. But, despite this growth, the contrast with Britain remained marked. Michael Harris has estimated that the weekly sale of London-produced papers in 1746 was around 100,000 (1987, p. 190). In the same year, there were around forty provincial papers in existence. If we assume an average sale for these papers of 300, which is probably on the low side, this would give a weekly sale of newspapers in England and Wales of around 112,000. The annual sale of London papers in 1780 has been estimated at around 16.6 million. If we assume that newspaper sales roughly tripled between 1746 and 1780, this would give us a national weekly sales figure of somewhere in the region of 340,000. Thus, the overall circulation of British papers in 1780 was greater than in France by a factor of between three and five, depending on one's estimate of overall circulations. This was in a population that was under a third the size, and an urban population under half the size. It is just worth noting that even if we included an estimate of sales of the provincial *affiches* in our figure for France, this would probably add less than 10,000 to the total.

What about readership? How does the social character of the readerships of the French and British press in the eighteenth century compare? We saw in a previous chapter that newspapers in Britain attracted a socially diverse readership, although the bulk of readers probably fell within the broad category of the middling ranks. As we would expect from the figures for circulation, newspapers in France had a more select readership. Direct evidence for this is sparse. Most surviving subscription lists are for literary or philosophical journals, the *Année littéraire, Journal étranger, Mercure de France, Journal helvétique*. The only exception is a list of subscribers for the Paris edition of *Gazette de France* for 1756 (Feyel, 1988). Of those subscribers whose status and occupation is listed, 31 per cent were from the titled nobility. Other groups significantly represented include high administration (*conseillers d'Etat, secrétaires du roi*, etc.), sovereign courts (Grand Conseil, Parlement, etc.), and finance and banking. In other words, they were concentrated towards the top of society. In the absence of other subscription lists, we are forced to make inferences about readership from the cost of papers and their content. The issue of cost is most easily dealt with. Most French newspapers were comparatively expensive. As far as foreign gazettes are concerned, this was part of the price that they had to pay for being tolerated by the French government and authorities. The annual subscription to the *Gazette de Leyde* was 36 livres which, as one historian has commented, was 'far more than a peasant or artisan could have spared' (Censer and Popkin, 1987, p. 86). William Doyle has suggested that the usual subscription for a journal in the 1760s, around 24 livres in Paris and 33 livres in the provinces, was around twice the weekly wage of a skilled worker (1989, p. 79). Papers that the French government was willing to encourage, or had greater control over, were cheaper. Annual subscription to the *Gazette de France* and the *Courrier d'Avignon* was 12 livres, while the cost of most provincial *affiches* was half as much again. This cost, however, would still have put them beyond the means of the vast bulk of the population. In England in the 1760s, the cost of annual purchase of a weekly paper was between two-thirds to just over one times the weekly wage of a skilled labourer (this rough estimate is based on wage levels for building craftsmen provided by Lindert and Williamson, 1982).

Content analysis presents more problems, not least because of the volume of material to be sampled as well as its diversity. In an important recent article, Stephen Botein, Jack Censer and Harriet Ritvo have compared social reportage and comment and advertising in a number of leading British and French metropolitan and provincial papers for selected years in the later eighteenth century (1981). They conclude that, in contrast to their British counterparts, 'periodicals in France continued to present an aristocratic view of society'. They link this to a more restricted readership, tighter political control and general conservatism. A partial exception to this trend was the provincial *affiches*, which had a much greater commercial content and were more obviously directed at a readership that encompassed merchants (see Censer, 1994, ch. 2; Jones, 1991, p. 92). Elsewhere, Popkin has analysed the advertisements carried in the *Gazette de Leyde* in the final third of 1787 in order to build up a fuller picture of the paper's readership (1989, pp. 131–2). The largest category of advertisements concerned investment opportunities and announcements directed at holders of government securities. A further quarter was placed by booksellers, and included a significant proportion referring to auctions of rare books. The rest referred to items for sale that fell within the purchasing power of those who, as Popkin puts it, possessed 'substantial discretionary incomes'. Caroll Joynes, mean-while, also looking at foreign gazettes, has emphasized the limitations in respect of readership suggested by a different aspect of their content. The gazettes, he observes, made little concession to ignorance among their readers. Rather, they assumed a high level of familiarity with events and issues (1987, p. 142): 'The audience was evidently expected to be familiar with, among other things, French and English constitutional history, Gallican ecclesiology, and canon law. There were no simplified explanations for the uninitiated, no summaries or recapitulations for latecomers.' In Britain, particularly after the 1770s, when the press gained the *de facto* right to report on the proceedings of Parliament, as we saw in the previous chapter, there was a definite trend towards clearer and more accessible coverage of political affairs.

The differences in readership between Britain and France undoubtedly partly reflected the respective nature of the elites in the two countries. The French upper ranks or notables, made up by the later eighteenth century of groups from the nobility, clergy and wealthy bourgeois, were more homogeneous and proportionately smaller than its British equivalent. It was this elite in France that was defining itself ever more closely in cultural terms from the 1750s and which lay behind the proliferation of provincial academies, literary societies, reading rooms and masonic lodges throughout provincial France in the same period (see esp. Mornet, 1967; Roche, 1978; Quéniart, 1978; Chartier, 1991). Another factor limiting newspaper readership in France under the old regime was the means by which most newspapers were disseminated. Unlike in Britain, where many newspapers were sold individually, the vast majority of papers in France were purchased by subscription. (This remained the case for most papers even after the Revolution.) There was some direct sale of papers, as Feyel has shown in respect of the *Gazette de France* (1988, p. 111). Feyel has also provided evidence for the practice of renting newspapers, either from the bureaux that dealt with subscriptions or street sellers. But in general, the mercuries and hawkers of London, the agents and newsmen of the provinces, so common throughout England, seem to have been a shadowy presence in the France of the old regime. A provincial reader of a French newspaper or gazette either had to contact the publisher or bureau in Paris dealing with distribution and sale directly or place an order through officers of the postal service.

A factor that might have extended the social range of French newspaper readership significantly was the provision of newspapers by provincial academies, literary societies, *cabinets littéraires*, cafés and shops. The extent to which this occurred under the old regime is an underexplored topic. A number of historians have emphasized the growth of a popular readership for news and pamphlets in Paris in this period (see esp. Roche, 1987, p. 220; see also Farge, 1994). For the 1780s, Louis-Sébastian de Mercier provides strong contemporary evidence for this. Of the capital's 600 cafés, Mercier observed, 'in most, the gossip is . . . boring: it is always about the Gazette'. Elsewhere he remarked of contemporary Parisians (quoted in Farge, 1994, p. 27):

There they are, sitting on a bench at the Tuileries, the Palais-Royal, the Arsenal, the Quai des Augustins or elsewhere. Three times a week they avidly read these sheets, and eagerness for political news has seized people of all ages and conditions.

Evidence for similar practices outside Paris is notably lacking. A number of historians have emphasized the spread of reading rooms in urban France (Roche, 1979). Jean Quéniart has traced this development in detail in southwest France (Quéniart, 1978). Nantes gained its first reading room in 1759. By 1788, the town possessed nine such institutions. Rennes got its first reading room in 1776. Between 1776 and 1789 it regularly subscribed to twenty-three different periodicals, including Linguet's *Annales*, the *Courrier de l'Europe* and the *Gazette de Leyde*, as well as to the official French newspapers. By the end of the old regime, any town of importance in the southwest had a reading room – Morlaix, Quimper, Dinan, Saint Malo, Brest and Angers. Subscription to reading rooms, however, was relatively expensive. At Rennes, the *droit d'entrée* was 27 livres in 1776 and 48 in 1783. On top of this a user had to pay an annual subscription of 24 livres. Censer has recently suggested that this sum excluded most people outside the sorts of groups that were already most likely to subscribe to periodicals and newspapers (1994, p. 190). Whether there was a level of newspaper readership below this, which remains to be uncovered by future historians, is unclear. Paul Benhamou has recently drawn attention to the spread of cheaper, less formal places where papers could be read from the 1770s (1992). This has led Pierre Rétat to talk of reading rooms becoming 'une phénomène de masse' in later eighteenth-century France (Duranton, Labrosse and Rétat, 1992, p. 132). In 1745, a police report on a Bordeaux bookseller described his shop as being a 'rendez-vous des nouvellistes'. The same report also commented: 'Il s'y trouve en conséquence beaucoup du monde tous les jours du courrier pour y apprendre les nouvelles' (quoted in McCleod, 1989, p. 265). Forty years later, an official in Avignon remarked (quoted in Moulinas, 1974, p. 363):

> Cette feuille maintient tout-à-fait son crédit et il m'a été assuré par des personnes qui fréquentent continuellement Marseille, que, dans les cafés et autres lieux publics ou les curieux se rassemblent pour les nouvelles, le Courrier d'Avignon est recherché de préference aux gazettes de France et d'Europe.

Such comments suggest that access to newspapers was possible for more than the upper ranks in larger towns in France before 1789.

Nevertheless, the general impression left by admittedly fragmentary evidence is that outlets for communal and popular readership of newspapers were fewer in number than across the Channel. In France there appears to have been no equivalent of the coffee house. As we have seen, the coffee houses or taverns and inns of urban Britain in this period served as major venues for newspaper readership among a wide cross-section of the upper and middling ranks. Foreign visitors tended to portray the coffee house as an aspect of a distinctive feature of eighteenth-century British society – the deep-rooted habits and practice of an urban conviviality that cut across many social barriers. Coffee houses and taverns also played a vital role in the construction of a national infrastructure of print in Britain. French reading rooms seem to have been notably different. Like the French press in general, they appear to have been less comercialized, and more elitist. How far they promoted political discussion and the transmission of political ideas and news is also difficult to determine. Baker has noted of illustrations of reading rooms, that their most striking aspect is the extent to which reading in them 'remains a solitary, private act' (Baker, 1987, p. 296). It was the French Revolution, and the emergence with it of a new political culture in France, that seems to have transformed collective habits of readership in towns other than Paris, at least so far as the political and newspaper press is concerned (see pp. 74, 77–8).

If patterns of readership seem to have differed significantly between Britain and France in the eighteenth century, similarly divergent were the commercial and business structures of newspapers. The details of this are beyond the scope of this work. What is worth emphasizing, however, is how the basic divergence created a very different set of relationships between the press and wider commercial trends and changes in France. Whereas in Britain, the general picture is of fierce competition, in France under the old regime access to the market was carefully controlled (Botein, Censer and Ritvo, 1981). The role (and importance) of advertising was also very different. Only the *affiches* in France were fully part of a wider process of commercialization (Jones, 1991). The foreign gazettes did, like the *affiches*, carry advertisements, but their cost and distance from French markets severely circumscribed their usefulness for advertising. This difference in respect of commercial structure was only reinforced after the French Revolution. The French papers of that era carried no advertisements; they were dependent on sales and subscriptions for their survival or profitability. They were also operating in a market that suddenly became much more open than that which operated across the Channel.

POLITICAL CONTROL AND POLITICS

One of the principal causes restricting the circulation of periodicals carrying political news and comment in France before 1789 was the elaborate system of political control exercised over the press. There is no general modern work on the ways in which this system affected the periodical press. It is nevertheless possible to piece together the outlines from various other sources. Although subject to certain limitations and of varying degrees of intensity at different stages during the century, official oversight of the press in France was a far more effective and imposing presence than political control in Britain. It also seems not to have been weakened to any significant degree before the confusion that overtook events in the final years before the Revolution.

As far as the periodical press was concerned, the ways in which the system operated differed for foreign gazettes on the one hand, and, on the other, publications produced in France. So far as the latter were concerned, their publication was controlled by a system of licensing and pre-publication censorship. The licences were, in effect, monopolies on particular types of publication, which were granted, in return for payment of a fee, usually to a consortium of individuals. The effect of this system was to create an interest among the various licensees in seeing that their monopolies were not illegally broken. Together with pre-publication censorship, this ensured that the political content of licensed Parisian papers (before 1778, the *Gazette* and, after that date, the *Mercure de France* and its supplement, the *Journal de Bruxelles*) was anodyne and uncontroversial. All historians agree that the licensed press fully upheld the official image of the French polity, that is of an absolute monarchy.

The foreign gazettes posed a much more interesting dilemma, the resolution of which was a classic example of the compromises and ambiguities that increasingly underpinned the old regime in France after the mid-century. The circulation of foreign gazettes certainly concerned the authorities, who were also sporadically pressurized by the official press to prevent their intrusion into France. Some time in the 1750s, Lamoignon de Malherbes, the *directeur de la Librairie* in France, composed a memorandum on the subject which exposed some of the problems that confronted ministers. Malherbes argued that to limit their intervention in domestic affairs, presumably by some form of pre-publication censorship, would be ineffective. As he wrote (quoted in Censer and Popkin, 1987, p. 84):

Such truncated gazettes would be purchased only by those people who could not obtain the real ones, and there are a thousand ways to smuggle in a printed sheet . . . and the gazetter, annoyed by a ban that would reduce his sales, would allow himself even more freedom.

Crude forms of control were attempted at various points in the 1770s and 1780s. The circulation of various gazettes was temporarily prohibited; editors were subject to intense diplomatic pressure. Such activity, however, tended not to last long, not least because it became bound up in rivalries between ministers. This last factor points to the essential feature of the mechanisms by which foreign gazettes were generally policed in France in this period – their informal nature.

As was referred to above, official toleration was conferred upon foreign gazettes in 1759 and their circulation systematized by the creation of a news agency in Paris to handle their distribution. This policy of 'tacit' approval appears to have worked to the authorities' advantage in that it gave them leverage over the papers. Only the most successful gazettes, with European readerships, the *Gazette de Leyde* and the *Gazette d'Amsterdam*, could afford to view the loss of access to the French market as anything less than disastrous. There were also collusive contacts between French ministers and the foreign gazettes. This might involve the provision of information. Certainly the foreign ministry seems to have had regular contact with the gazettes. Towards the end of the old regime, ministerial rivalries also seem to have spilled over into the pages of certain foreign gazettes. Popkin, for example, has noted that the *Gazette de Leyde* was exploited between 1787 and 1788 by opponents of Calonne (1987). During the Diamond Necklace affair of 1785, the same paper was used by the court to publicize its version of the affair (Popkin, 1989, pp. 194–5).

If the ministry tried to weaken the potential problems posed by the foreign gazettes through toleration, it also sought to undermine their influence in other ways. At various points during the century, ministers sponsored papers that were ostensibly independent of the French authorities to promote views favourable to the court and the monarchy. Perhaps the most successful example of 'covert' intervention was the *Courrier d'Avignon*. This paper circulated widely in the southern half of France (Moulinas, 1974, pp. 361–2). But it was totally dependent for its success and sales on preferential treatment granted by the French postal services and, through them, the tacit permission of the French foreign ministry. The paper's modern historian, René Moulinas, refers to the potential withdrawal of this as a 'sword of Damocles' hanging over the paper's head. The extent of official favour shown to the paper went further than this. Rival papers were suppressed; royal officials sought to promote its readership. The *quid pro quo* was that the paper represented

French politics and policy in a light that was favourable to the ministry and court, which, on the whole, it did. Censer has emphasized that it did carry material that could have been seen as problematic for the French ministry and that coverage of foreign affairs was not always positive, as was the case during the Seven Years War. But the reality of French control is symbolized by the fact that when a new lease for the paper was negotiated in 1778, the talks took place in Paris and not Rome or Avignon. They also took place under the scrutiny of the French foreign minister, the Comte de Vergennes.

The oversight of the *Courrier d'Avignon* represents only one of a number of attempts to promote favourable publicity and news by French ministers. In the early 1770s, René Maupeou and the Duc d'Aiguillon tried supporting the tri-monthly *Journal historique et politique* to counteract the gazettes, but this was unsuccessful. The *Courrier de Bas-Rhin*, published in the duchy of Cleves, and generally authoritarian in its views, was subsidized by the French court to the extent of 4,800 subscriptions. The triumvirate – Maupeou, Terray and d'Aiguillon – allowed Pankcoucke to publish two periodicals in France that purported to be produced outside its borders – the *Journal de Bruxelles* and the *Journal de Genève*. After 1775, Vergennes was particularly active in ensuring that French policy towards the American Independence and the war between America (and subsequently France) and Britain received favourable coverage. This involved not only attempts, partially successful, to influence papers like the *Gazette de Leyde*, but also the sponsorship of a number of papers published abroad. The *Courrier de l'Europe* was established independently of the French court in 1776. Soon after its first appearance, an article critical of the French government and Vergennes, Maurepas and Marie Antoinette caused its entry into France to be prohibited. This prohibition was lifted, but only after intervention by Beaumarchais. The paper was from henceforth subject to close censorship. Beaumarchais also acted as an intermediary between the paper and Vergennes. In 1778, when the British government threatened action against the paper, the French authorities even allowed an edition to be published at Boulogne.

These attempts to influence debate in France by ministers provide another fascinating insight into some of the limitations surrounding control of the press in this period and the ways in which broadly disseminated Enlightenment attitudes restricted ministers' scope for action. It was generally recognized that, to gain a wide hearing, ministerial views and propaganda had to appear to come from a reasonably independent source. Openly acknowledged official sources would have little impact. A text submitted to Vergennes in the hand of a foreign office official highlighted the dilemma facing ministers. The official described unsuccessful attempts during the Seven Years War to establish an official organ in the press, and continued (quoted in Sgard, 1991, vol. i, p. 5):

> les temps actuels demanderaient plus de circonspection et une système différent, puisqu'autre chose et sur les ennemis, ou de parler des affaires d'une nation avec laquelle on vit en bonne intelligence l'essence de celui-ci servait qu'on le crût une production tolérée de quelque anonyme. Il s'y joindrait l'avantage d'une ressource quelque fois précieuse à la politique, je veux dire avoir une véhicule tout prêt pour des insinuations ou des observations qui perdraient leurs effet dans les écrits avoués ou privilégiés.

Moulinas has written elsewhere of the need for the ministry to reconcile the principle of official control of the press with the practical exigencies of shaping contemporary opinion (1974, p. 389). This required an attitude on the part of ministers that was, as Moulinas puts it, 'full of duplicity'.

If the basic outlines of press control in France can be established, the details of policy, its exact aims, and changes over time, are far more difficult to establish in detail. The importance of the latter has recently been emphasized by Censer, as have the gaps in our current knowledge of this aspect of political control (1994, ch. 5). Perhaps the most important point to emerge from Censer's examination of these issues is the success of press control in France towards the end of the old regime. Far from there being a secular trend towards increasing independence of the press, as in Britain, in France press control was far more effectively applied in the 1780s than in the 1750s or 1760s. Both Malherbes, who largely oversaw policy towards the press in the early 1750s, and the Duc de Choiseul, who was the guiding force from the later 1750s, showed considerable latitude in intervening against both domestic and foreign-produced papers. The result was that, particularly in certain foreign gazettes, there was considerable publicity given to opponents of the court. By contrast, the triumvirate were almost completely successful in stifling press criticism between 1771 and 1774. As Popkin has written, the *Gazette de Leyde*, the most troublesome of the foreign gazettes, 'could [during this period] do little more than print the official edicts put out by the ministers and the remodeled "Maupeou parlements"' (1989, p. 140). The fall of the triumvirate saw a temporary relaxation of press control. This came to an end, however, towards the end of 1776, and was followed by a new phase of tighter control until 1784. Helped by widespread enthusiasm for France's role in the War of American Independence,

Vergennes succeeded in policing the press with remarkable effect. How much this owed also to a calmer political atmosphere is difficult to judge. The late 1770s and early 1780s did not see the clashes between the court and the *parlements* that periodically animated political debate in France between the 1750s and mid-1770s. As a number of historians have demonstrated, in so far as new forms of politics and new political languages were taking root in old-regime France, the *parlements*, through their right to publish remonstrances, were instrumental. With regard to press control, little is known about the final years of the old regime, although Popkin's work on the *Gazette de Leyde* suggests considerable confusion, with no single line of policy being consistently pursued. Whatever the precise role and aims of ministers and the court, the press regained much of the vigour that has characterized it in the 1750s and 1760s.

During the second half of the eighteenth century, then, the intensity of control of the press varied. But how should we, in general terms, characterize the intervention of particularly the foreign gazettes in French politics during this period? One historian has referred to a 'press revolution' beginning at the mid-century (Joynes, 1987, p. 167). This overstates the case. There are two sides to the question. The first is concerned with the content of the gazettes, with the range of comment and information that they were able to provide on controversial events and decisions. The second concerns their symbolic role, the meanings that contemporaries attached to their presence in French political life. The question of the range of political news and views carried in the gazettes is difficult to answer very fully, given the current state of research. The paper about which most is known is the *Gazette de Leyde*. Caroll Joynes has examined its coverage of the conflict between Louis XV and the *parlements* in the 1750s. The picture he draws is of a paper that was engaging seriously, and in a partisan way, with events. As he comments (1987, p. 142):

> The reports [in the paper] communicated the urgency and seriousness of the situation, which contrasted starkly with the effect of the spare almost clinical prose employed in previous decades (and even in the 1750s when dealing with the rest of Europe).

Popkin has drawn a similar picture of the paper in the final crises of the old regime, stressing also its role in disseminating many of the ideological concepts – for example, constitutionalism, national sovereignty – that had such a formative (or perhaps destabilizing) role to play after 1789 (1989). It is less clear how far this sort of journalism was practised outside specific political crises and in other foreign gazettes.

Censer has written of the *Courrier d'Avignon* of the 1770s (1987, p. 179): 'The periodical provided no editorials or general interpretative articles to guide the reader, but only a pastiche of geographical perspectives and a multitude of facts.' A detailed study of the coverage by the press of the Damiens affair in 1758 (Robert Damiens attempted to assassinate Louis XV in 1757 and was executed the following year) has emphasized the 'prudence' of not just domestic periodicals but also the foreign gazettes (Rétat, 1979). Damiens's statements were ignored and no connection was made, except by the *Gazette de Leyde*, with important contemporary events such as the crisis created by the refusal of sacraments to priests of Jansenist leanings or the conflict between the King and the Parlement of Paris. Rather the attempted assassination was portrayed as the action of an isolated maniac. What makes such silences all the more significant is the fact that alternative, highly politicized interpretations of the affair were current in Paris at the time (Kaplan, 1984). Even in the case of the *Gazette de Leyde*, we need to be careful about not exaggerating the directness of its approach to political questions. The editorial policy was 'not blatant', as one historian has written. The same historian has also commented: 'either *consciously or unconsciously*, the *Gazette*'s editor was encouraging the development of public opinion' (my italics) (Popkin, 1987, pp. 166, 167).

This last statement is important because it focuses on the ambiguities of the coverage of politics in the foreign gazettes, on what they were not, rather than what they were. The journalistic standards of the paper were those of an elite journal of record. Their aim was to present as full and accurate a coverage of events as they could. This disposition was exposed very clearly at the beginning of the French Revolution. They displayed considerable caution in 1789 – one of the reasons that they were rapidly overtaken in popularity by the burgeoning and bolder indigenous press after July of that year (see Popkin, 1991). On 21 July 1789 the editor of the *Gazette de Leyde* told his readers that he would be withholding reports of rumoured events in Paris (a reference to the fall of the Bastille) because he did not want to relay rumours 'of blood spilled by the troops in the middle of the capital and all the horrors that presage civil war' without confirmation of their truth.

As already mentioned, it has also been argued that the gazettes had a symbolic importance over and above their practical functions. What is meant by this seems to be two slightly different things. First, that by tolerating their existence ministers implied that the public had a right to know about political affairs and even a right to put forward a view about them. In doing so, it has also been argued that they gave substance to the emerging concept of public opinion. Second, the papers embodied an image of political life that was seriously at odds with official ideology. In their presentation of politics, in their portrayal of the *parlements* as the equivalent of American colonial assemblies, they offered a vision of a 'politics of contestation', a politics in which decisions were the outcome of debate and argument. One major problem with the above arguments is that they are inherently untestable. We simply do not know whether contemporaries drew these sorts of conclusions based on their existence. As Denis Richet has suggested, we should also be careful about appearing to paint too crude a picture of political life in previous periods and beyond the reach of the gazettes (1991). Political divisions existed before the gazettes emerged, as did means to communicate them, such as rumour, images, manuscript newsletters, posters, handbills, demonstrations, or the pulpit. As Rétat has recently observed of the dissemination of parliamentary edicts in Paris in 1788, 'c'est par la bouche à oreille dans les cafés et dans les parcs que se diffusait le message d'ensemble de ces déclarations' (1989, p. 14). Establishing that the gazettes did carry various possible messages is not the same as establishing their influence. In this context, we might also note that the great political debate that accompanied the calling of the Estates General in 1789 was conducted in pamphlets and not in newspapers. And despite the advantages of the latter as means of political communication, their ability to construct strong linkages between a dispersed public, the Third Estate were able to display remarkable levels of political coordination and common purpose. As Eisenstein has written (1990, p. 155), 'however important was the role of the periodical press in shaping events after 1789, it was largely without its aid that the French body politic was reconstituted between 1788 and 1789'.

In political life, then, as in so many other areas, the comparison with the British press again seems very marked. This could be demonstrated in many ways, in terms of styles of journalism, the degree of political control over the press, or perhaps even more importantly, the ways in which the press interacted with various facets of contemporary political life. In Britain, as we saw in an earlier chapter, the press helped to shape, in both a practical and ideological manner, the various forms of public politics that crystallized in the course of the century. It was of vital importance in the promotion of organized expressions of opinion. In this way and in others, it linked very firmly the political worlds of the localities to political institutions, activities and events at the centre. It did not stand back from politics; it was itself an important political actor. In France, largely because of the degree of political control, the intervention of even the foreign gazettes took place on a more detached and abstract level. Political divisions may have occasionally been reflected in the press, but they were not obviously manipulated or directly encouraged. At certain important moments, the foreign gazettes reported on the political battles that were being fought out between the *parlements* and the courts. As part of an attempt to provide as full a coverage of events as possible, they reproduced parliamentary remonstrances, as well as pro-parliamentary propaganda. But they always did this within a series of partly self-imposed journalistic conventions that consigned them to a primarily passive role in political life. They were unable, or did not seek to apply pressure, to shape opinion in overt ways. As Popkin has written, 'the requirements for survival in old-regime Europe severely limited the ways in which newspapers could represent the events of the day' (1991, p. 98).

THE FRENCH REVOLUTION AND THE PRESS

Between 1788 and 1789, as the old regime in France collapsed, so did the old controls over the press (Labrosse and Rétat, 1989). This freedom was confirmed in the 1791 constitution, and lasted, in varying degrees, until 1797, when the Directory started seriously to undermine the freedom of the press. Freedom is relative, and during the various phases of the Revolution changing political conditions shaped the experiences of the press and journalists. Press freedom was at its greatest between July 1789 and the summer of 1792. The massacre of the Champ de Mars triggered a crackdown against a number of extremist papers, but it was only after the taking of the Tuileries and the fall of the French monarchy that the first serious restriction of press freedom occurred, with the suppression of right-wing papers. Press freedom was severely compromised during the Terror and many journalists either fled or were executed. The fall of Robespierre brought some relaxation of control, and right-wing papers once more emerged. The constitution of 1795 temporarily restricted press freedom, but it was a law of 22 Fructidor (8 September 1797), providing for the deportation of journalists, editors and owners of papers, that commenced a gradual return to conditions of tight control in France, a process that culminated under Napoleon.

From July 1789, the French press burst into life. There was an 'explosion of print'. In 1789 alone, roughly 100 new papers sprang into life (Rétat, 1989). Between May 1789 and October 1791 a total of 515 papers were published in Paris (Censer, 1976, pp. 9–10). Overall circulation multiplied many times over. At the height of the Revolution, Popkin has estimated that there was an upper limit of around 300,000 copies per day being produced in Paris alone (1990, p. 83). The circulation of successful individual papers did not in most cases exceed the totals reached during the old regime. One recent estimate suggests that an influential paper in this period usually had a print run of between 2,000 and 5,000 (Gilchrist and Murray, 1971, p. 9). Most of the overall expansion in circulation was owing to the multiplication of titles. A few papers, however, were printed in unprecedentedly high numbers (for this, and a summary of existing information on circulation figures for revolutionary papers, see Chisick, 1992, pp. 21–6). The *Révolutions de Paris* may, for certain issues, have had a circulation of around 200,000, although this was an exceptional case. The *Feuille villageoise*, a paper that aimed to bring the message of the Revolution to the countryside, reached a peak circulation of around 15,000. The various versions of the radical paper *Père Duchesne* probably circulated in numbers approaching 100,000. The majority of papers had far lower circulations, especially the hundreds that survived only for a handful of issues.

The effect of the Revolution on the provincial press was less straightforward. As Popkin has recently remarked, the number of provincial papers appearing at any one time was not much greater than the number published at the end of the old regime (1993a). This reflected the simple fact that most of the demand fuelling the proliferation of newspapers in this period was demand for news of events in Paris. The force of this demand changed the nature of the provincial press; it became more like most of its Parisian counterparts, carrying news and political comment. Obviously, papers produced in Paris had better and earlier access to this news. Provincial papers, at best, could only offer weekly digests of Paris papers at a lower cost than subcription to one or more daily Paris journals. Nevertheless, aggregate figures disguise a huge amount of press activity in the provinces. Gough has counted 167 new provincial titles launched between the beginning of 1789 and the end of the Constituent Assembly's sessions in September 1791 (1988, p. 76). Between 1789 and 1799, seventy-nine different titles were produced in Bordeaux, thirty-nine in Lyon, thirty-three in Rouen, over thirty in Strasbourg and twenty-two in Angers. Most of these new papers, however, like many of their Parisian counterparts, were extremely short-lived. Of Gough's 167 papers, only eighty-five lasted for more than three months, and only forty-five for more than a year.

The contrast between the old-regime press and the revolutionary press is, therefore, stark. After July 1789, the volume of political news and comment carried in the press took off. The readership of newspapers also changed substantially. Popkin has suggested that the new readership 'constituted a larger proportion of the total population than had ever been included in political life in any other country' (1990, p. 65). Most individual subscribers to most newspapers continued to be drawn from the relatively well-off, although surviving subscription lists do provide confirmation of increased readership of papers among artisans and shopkeepers (Chisick, 1992, esp. p. 210). It was, however, changes in the collective and public reading of papers that almost certainly extended the social range of newspaper readership most. Michael Kennedy has emphasized the strength of the relationship between the Jacobin clubs and the press (1982, pp. 53–77; 1984). Clubs not merely subscribed to large numbers of newspapers, they also held public readings. The press was at the very centre of political debate and discussions in the clubs. The more formal and regular proceedings of the clubs were mirrored by informal readings, such as the tobacconist who read from a paper every day outside his shop in Caen. The result of all this activity was, as Christine Peyraud has written in respect of provincial readership: 'l'opinion publique n'est plus circonscrite à une élite lettrée et urbaine mais englobe les couches populaires de la ville et de la campagne' (1989, p. 462).

If there were many new newspaper readers in France between 1789 and 1799, we should be careful not to exaggerate the social and geographical reach of the press. There is, for example, ample room for scepticism about how far the press penetrated the countryside, especially among the peasantry. The most successful of the instruction papers of the Revolution, the *Feuille villageoise*, was aimed at this section of society, but modern studies have indicated that it reached more city dwellers than true peasants. In so far as it did penetrate the countryside, it was through the clergy. An analysis of published letters in its pages has shown that fully 57 per cent were from priests (Popkin, 1990, p. 87). Illiteracy was one barrier to press readership in rural France; language was another. Most French peasants did not speak French, but a form of patois. Language was also a major barrier to the readership of papers among France's linguistic minorities in various border provinces. The one exception to this generalization was the German-speaking population of Strasbourg which did have access to a newspaper press in its own language. The importance of newspaper readership among the Parisian Sans-Culottes has also been questioned. Albert Soboul found some examples of public readership of papers among the Sans-Culottes, but concluded that few read the papers explicitly aimed at them on a regular basis (1958, p. 672). Harvey Chisick has recently suggested that first-hand accounts of political activity at this level show that the printed word played a relatively unimportant role in forming perceptions and influencing action. Chisick cites the example of the glazier, Jacques-Louis Ménétra, who was literate, but who had few contacts with printed books. As Chisick remarks (1991a, p. 372): 'His descriptions of the politics of the *sections* and his life in Paris during the Revolution reflect a world in which local friendships or rivalries were decisive, and in which political and cultural interaction were overwhelmingly oral.' As Chisick also observes, building a case on one individual is insufficient. It is also the case that, as Arlette Farge has shown for old-regime Paris, and as was the case in eighteenth-century Britain, print and oral culture interacted at many points (1994). Marat's journalistic tirades were no doubt retailed and endlessly transmuted by word of mouth. But the essential point remains: the revolutionary press was part of a dense skein of communications of which print was only one element.

Whatever the limitations of newspaper readership, from July 1789 the French press nevertheless developed from being proportionately much smaller and weaker than its British counterpart to a point where it was appearing on a scale that far exceeded the British press. The question of how far, and in what ways, this expanded and transformed press influenced the French Revolution is one that has produced little agreement among historians. Many historians have sought to pass over the issue, preferring instead to focus on the press as a guide to the fluctuating opinions, ideologies and *mentalités* that accompanied the several phases of the Revolution. Among those historians who have attempted to address the issue, many have produced notably ambiguous answers. Popkin, who is among those historians most anxious to assert a distinctive role and influence for the press, suggests that its record was a 'mixed one' (1990, p. 142). Like other historians, he acknowledges that there is no evidence that the crises of the Revolution were significantly influenced by the press. But the press, he maintains, was nevertheless a 'vital constituent of the revolutionary atmosphere'; it helped to create and maintain an atmosphere of 'tension and hope'. The most original interpretation of the role of the press in this period has been put forward by Rétat (1985). Rétat has argued that the revolutionary press, by its proximity to events and its ability to report and comment on them on a daily basis, was able to create a new relationship between readers and events. Readers could be made to feel part of the drama of revolutionary events. Newspapers also gave these events a shape, and sense of continuity. In this way, Rétat suggests, newspapers transformed events into symbolic episodes; they gave them meaning. This ability to create a coherent narrative out of isolated events and episodes made revolution conceivable. In this admittedly somewhat ambiguous and complex sense, the press created the Revolution.

Rétat's thesis is suggestive without being conclusive, but again it underlines the gap between the old-regime press and the revolutionary press. Under the conditions created by the Revolution, Paris became the centre of the French newspaper world in a way that political control had prevented under the old regime. The foreign gazettes rapidly lost their influence (and readership) (Popkin, 1990). The style of news reportage changed in significant ways. Journalists were close to the events that they were describing. Often they were participants in these events. Reports had a new immediacy; they spoke directly to their readers. Under the old regime, news and comment on domestic political events had to be sent outside the country before returning in the pages of the foreign gazettes. As Censer has remarked, 'News always seemed to come from far away' (1994, p. 18).

Changes in the press after 1789 are easily described. Not so easily formulated are general conclusions about its changed influence. The problems are substantial. One of the most obvious (and important) is the astonishing diversity of the revolutionary press. This was one of its most striking features, and can be related both to the ease of entry into the press market as well as the absence of political consensus in France, particularly after 1791 (Chisick, 1992; Popkin, 1990). Diversity was more than just a matter of papers of very different political viewpoints. It was also a consequence of different forms of paper and very different journalistic styles. Journals of record, such as those that specialized in reporting the actions and debates of the National and Constituent Assemblies and the Convention – the *Moniteur*, the *Journal logographique*, or the *Bulletin de la convention nationale* – were produced with very different ends in mind to papers of instruction – the *Feuille villageoise* or the *Manuel du laboureur et de l'artisan*, a paper instituted by a Marseilles radical which comprised weekly conversations between peasants and a fictional rustic sage 'Anselme' – or narrowly polemical papers – the short-lived satirical papers of the right wing in 1791 or the inflammatory papers of the Parisian radicals and *enragés*, Desmoulins's *Les Révolutions de Paris et Brabant*, Brissot's *Patriote française*, or Marat's *Ami du peuple*. Some papers were produced in poster form, or with headlines and summaries to be cried out by street sellers. Successive factions sponsored papers, dispatching them, at no cost to the recipients, to the provinces in large numbers. Most papers, however, had to depend on their success in the marketplace. There were significant differences in the language and vocabulary employed by journalists. As Popkin has emphasized, this is even true of radical papers aimed at a popular audience (1990, esp. pp. 145–68). Marat's sensationalist writing in his *Ami du peuple* was very different to that of Hébert in his famous paper the *Père Duchesne*. Marat's language was 'severely classical'; he made no attempt to write in the language of the people. Hébert's journal was not only written in a deliberately vulgar and popular style, it was also designed to look like popular literature.

Another major problem is that the Revolution transformed other media of political communication at the same time as changing the nature and scale of the press. Lynn Hunt, who has written extensively on the new political culture created by the French Revolution, while recognizing the transformation in the press, has emphasized the degree of innovation in that culture independent of the press (1984, pp. 19–20). Songs, cartoons, handbills, posters, festivals, processions, demonstrations, political clubs – all were constituent elements of a political culture in an unexampled state of flux and development. Against this background of a kaleidoscope of voices and images, distinguishing the impact of the press from other media is extremely difficult.

Nevertheless, there is some evidence that can be brought to bear that suggests some of the limitations surrounding the impact of the press in this period, as well as pointing to some of the ways in which the press did contribute distinctively to revolutionary political culture. This evidence concerns the relationship between Jacobin clubs and the press. Kennedy has described the relationship between the two as 'symbiotic'. As he comments: 'Virtually every club subscribed to at least one paper, some took over 20' (1984, p. 476). Meetings in smaller organizations often consisted almost entirely of reading periodicals. Clubs organized public readings. Members used periodicals to instruct and animate groups among the population outside the clubs. Some clubs supported provincial papers, although the enthusiasm for this activity was usually not matched by results. Such papers tended to be very short-lived (Gough, 1991). Perhaps the most interesting feature of the clubs' relationship with the press, however, is the way in which clubs selected the papers to which they subscribed. Although some clubs did subscribe to papers with views opposed to their own, most only read polemical papers whose views they found congenial. Papers that began to express views with which the clubs were out of sympathy quickly found themselves disgarded. This is what happened, for example, to the *Journal de Paris* after October 1791, when it began to show definite right-wing sympathies (Kennedy, 1984, p. 478). The pattern was to repeat itself again and again before 1794, as the political complexion of papers and of the clubs shifted. This aspect of club behaviour suggests that, in many cases, the revolutionary press may have played a greater role in buoying the spirits of the already politically committed than in persuading the neutral or the unconverted. Subscription list evidence tends to support this. Thus, a list for the conservative *Ami du Roi* for 1791 shows that around 47 per cent of subscriptions where occupation or status is specified were accounted for by the clergy (Chisick, 1992, p. 210). Harvey Chisick's analysis of subscriptions to the official journal of the Jacobin regime of 1793–4, the *Journal de la*

Montagne, is even more suggestive. More than 80 per cent of collective subscriptions were from popular societies or Jacobin clubs. Forty per cent of the individual subscribers whose occupations are known were engaged in state service. Of those that identified themselves by member-ship of irregular government agencies, thirty-four were members of *sociétés populaires* and fifteen sat on *comités de surveillance*. Chisick has concluded that 'subscribers to the *Journal de la Montagne* were generally well off, and actively engaged in supporting the Revolution' (Chisick, 1991a). Popkin's analysis of a number of right-wing papers from the Directory period only underlines the tendency of revolutionary papers to appeal to those who already shared the perspectives and principles of these papers (1980, pp. 54–83).

Such a conclusion does not mean that the revolutionary press did not have important effects. Like the press in Britain, it was undoubtedly an important means by which groups of politically like-minded individuals came to see themselves as part of a wider movement. A number of Jacobin papers were primarily designed to provide a vehicle for correspondence between the Jacobin club in Paris and its provincial affiliates. The Jacobins of Saint-Jean-de-Luz wrote to the Paris society to say that 'La lecture de vos débats et de votre correspondance nous instruit de tout de qui passé dans l'empire' (quoted in Kennedy, 1984, p. 482). Right-wing papers also solicited contributions from readers. As Popkin has suggested, in providing this linkage the press had advantages over other forms of printed propaganda. These advantages included continuity and the opportunity for amplification and correction, as well as the ability of the press to provide a forum for the exchange of views. By providing a focus for political allegiance, the press also helped to harden political divisions and antagonisms. It served to define political positions more starkly, helping to fix political stereotypes and images. In an entirely different context, Sean Connolly has recently referred to the ways in which party conflict in early eighteenth-century Ireland took on its own momentum. Much political conflict, Connolly also reminds us, took place (and still takes place) at a symbolic level. And as Connolly remarks, 'Because so much conflict took place at this symbolic level . . . it was easy for each party to attribute to the other principles more extreme than the majority at least of its members actually supported' (Connolly, 1992, p. 81). During the French Revolution, papers became concrete symbols of partisanship. In many places, papers were publicly burnt to signify disapproval or hostility, and journalists were visited by hostile mobs. The press helped to recast political life into simple and intelligible patterns.

Finally, there is the less easily resolved but still vital question of the importance of the news carried by the press. The desire for news was the major force behind the expansion of the press after 1789. Jacobin clubs, almost without exception, subscribed to at least one paper that provided what they thought of as accurate and up-to-date news of events in Paris (Kennedy, 1982, pp. 53–77). When papers failed to arrive on time, postal officials were the object of vigorous complaints. There was an eagerness to receive the latest news. By keeping many different groups and parts of the country informed about events on a fairly continous basis, the press helped, as Rétat has suggested, to create a common revolutionary drama. It reinforced the linkages between local events and national events; it helped to provide a common frame of reference for their interpretation. This was a distinctive contribution. No other medium or mechanism could have done it with anywhere near the same effectiveness or comprehensiveness.

CONCLUSIONS

The French press under the old regime presented a stark contrast to its counterpart in Britain. The British press was not only circulated on a far larger scale and through a broader cross-section of society before 1789, it played a very different role in the political culture of Britain. The influence of the press in old-regime France was less direct, and because of this is more difficult to pin down. Its role in providing information on political events and personalities, and in opening up the political system to different interpretations and closer public scrutiny, was tightly circumscribed as late as the mid-1780s. Indeed it was more closely restricted from 1776 to 1784 than it had been in the 1750s and 1760s.

As in so many other spheres, the Revolution completely changed the nature and role of the press in France. Some historians have sought to downplay or qualify this perception in recent years, but at best they have done no more than qualify it marginally. As William Murray has recently emphasized, papers producing 'news as they saw it, analysed without fear or favour, and presented as they thought appropriate' were 'one of the first creations' of the Revolution (1986, p. 170). The distance between the press and politics also narrowed to the point at which it was, perhaps paradoxically, closer than it had ever been across the Channel. The impact on political life of the new, revolutionary press did show some similarities with its British counterpart, although crucial differences of degree existed. As in Britain, the revolutionary press helped to harden political divisions and antagonisms; it provided a vehicle for groups in different parts of the country to speak to one another; it provided a common language and framework for understanding political events and developments. Urbanization also continued to exercise a close influence on the fortunes of the press, particularly in respect of readership and dissemination. But here the comparison ends. Revolutionary papers were very different in commercial structure to their British counterparts. Most were far less stable; they were less integrated in the commercial life of the country; they contained no advertisements. If a remotely similar press had ever existed in Britain it was during the civil wars of the previous century, when newsbooks had helped to create populist modes of discourse, and when they had also played an important role in stabilizing and giving temporary shape to an extremely unstable popular opinion.

4 The press, society and political culture

This chapter explores relationships between the press and political culture (broadly defined) as well as various social and cultural boundaries and divisions. The role of the press in these contexts is attracting increasing attention from historians. This reflects deeper shifts in historical debate, in particular a growing interest in exploring the ideas, languages (discourses) and habits that helped to create the sense that people were able to make of social orders and political realities in the past. While it is recognized that these factors and experiences were not uninfluenced by economic realities, many historians argue that these did not dictate their nature or the meanings that contemporaries found in them (for this, see esp. Corfield, 1991). This growing body of work, and the assumptions that underpin it, pose a series of challenges for historians of the press. In particular, they point to a picture of the press as an active force in history, as something that intervened in social, cultural and political relationships, as well as being shaped by them.

The main focus of this chapter is on England, Wales and Scotland, although comparisons will be made with France at certain points. The conclusions put forward are somewhat tentative and suggestive. Furnishing a full picture of the relationship between the pre-1800 press and the changing social, cultural and political horizons is a task that is currently beyond us. In a number of crucial areas relevant research is lacking or sparse. Perhaps most importantly, detailed work on the social and cultural identity of the growing middling ranks in Britain is only just beginning to appear, and, as yet, nothing like a consensus has emerged on how best to portray that identity or those identities (but see Langford, 1989; Wahrman, 1992a; Money, 1993; Smail, 1994; Nenadic, 1988, 1990). Close analysis of the content of most papers, particularly for the later eighteenth century, is also lacking (although see Barker, 1994). The approach here is also selective. A number of specific relationships have been singled out for closer examination. These are the relationships between the press and, first, national, regional and local identities, and second, changing perceptions of social and cultural identity among the propertied classes. Finally, the contribution of the press in both Britain and France to the development of the concept of a free press as a political value is briefly examined. The choice of these relationships has been determined by their importance, and by the weight that a number of historians have recently placed upon them.

THE PRESS AND NATIONAL INTEGRATION

That the growth of the press in Britain and France was a powerful force for national integration, at a cultural, social and political level, is generally accepted, although just how powerful is more difficult to pin down. The importance of the press in this context owed much to the relationships between different elements of the press. As we have already seen, the subordination of provincial and Scottish papers to the London press only grew during the eighteenth century. Provincial and Scottish papers did not exist primarily to provide information about local events. Readers could be expected to have other forms of access to local information and news. What they sought from their provincial paper was a summary of the contents of the London papers. It was only at the very end of our period that the volume of local material carried in some provincial and Scottish papers began to grow significantly. In many instances, this was a case simply of more of the same; provincial papers in the first half of the eighteenth century had carried occasional articles of local topographical and antiquarian interest; they had also carried sporadic items about local social events, charities, crime and court cases. In so far as there was definite change, it was in the amount of locally inspired political material. This is a reflection of the changing nature of public politics, a development in which, as we saw in an earlier chapter, the provincial press was closely involved.

A few, principally literary or cultural, papers became important symbols of metropolitan culture. This was above all true of the *Spectator*, undoubtedly the most influential literary paper of the eighteenth century, not just in Britain but throughout Europe. Yet as John Clive has written with reference to Scotland (1970, p. 225), it was not just avowed arbiters of taste like the *Spectator* that were carriers of metropolitan standards and views. It was true of all types of paper (see the discussion of this in the contemporary American colonial context in Clark, 1994). It was also a feature of many newspapers that became increasingly obvious in the final decades of the eighteenth century. From the 1770s, a growing number of provincial papers paid substantial attention to metropolitan fashion. In the 1770s, the *Leeds Mercury* regularly included an item entitled 'The Dress of the Month', which suggests a significant female readership or at least a perception on the part of the printer that this existed. Interestingly, much of the attention to fashion focused on the court, which seems to support Linda Colley's recent suggestion that there was a definite shift in attitudes in Britain towards the royal family and its role in social and political perceptions from around the 1780s (Colley, 1984). Unlike in the first half of the century, most newspapers in the 1780s and 1790s included detailed descriptions of court functions, such as the celebrations and balls on royal birthdays. These descriptions included minutely detailed accounts of the various clothes worn by the leading members of the court. In its social comment more generally, the press also took its cue from London, not least because of the influence of the London press on the provincial and Scottish press.

The role of advertising in the provincial and Scottish press also takes on an additional significance in this context. Advertising was a feature of press content that again became more and more important in the second half of the eighteenth century, although the initial growth of newspaper advertising can be traced to the late 1730s and early 1740s. In the 1710s and 1720s, advertisements in provincial papers were generally few in number and often only one or two lines in length. In 1717, the *Worcester Post Man* had an average of two advertisements per issue. Representative was the following advertisement: 'All sorts of Colours, Varnishes, Brushes, and Pencils for Painters, are sold at Mr Harry Pitt's, an Apothecary in Goose Lane, Worcester.' By the end of the century, advertisements covered between a quarter and a half of the space in most papers. In the early 1780s, nearly two pages of the eight-page paper the *Edinburgh Advertiser* were devoted to advertisements. In the 1730s, the *Salisbury Journal* carried an annual average of 296 advertisements. In 1770, this figure had risen to over 3,300 (Ferdinand, 1993, p. 398). The majority of advertisements were also longer and more elaborate, often involving a considerable amount of text, headings and subheadings, and, in some cases, illustrations. A growing proportion emphasized the fact that the goods they were bringing to the attention of the reader represented the latest London fashions. Neil McKendrick has suggested the importance of capturing the London market in luxury goods as a basis from which to tackle rapidly growing provincial markets (McKendrick, 1982; although see also Styles, 1993). The focus of McKendrick's work has been Josiah Wedgewood, the great pottery manufacturer, but, as he also argues, many lesser traders also took advantage of the same prejudices or cultural imperatives.

Advertisements emphasizing the London provenance of goods were a stock-in-trade of many provincial shopkeepers. Purveyors of services to the wealthier classes – architects, estate surveyors, portrait painters, gardeners, decorative plasterers – also used the press to boast about their metropolitan origins, connections or training. The message that these advertisements powerfully conveyed was that London was synonymous with fashionable taste.

In France, as a number of historians have shown, the expansion of the periodical press from the 1730s also served to reinforce cultural integration among the elites in society (see esp. Mornet, 1967; Chartier, 1991; Bellanger *et al.*, 1969; Censer, 1994). In this, literary and philosophical papers complemented other literary forms, such as books and pamphlets, which were circulated in ever greater numbers during the century (see esp. Darnton, 1982). Because of their local provenance and their role in giving expression to local opinion and views, the *affiches*, the equivalent of English provincial papers, may have had a more distinctive contribution to make. As we saw in the previous chapter, the establishment of the *affiches* was a development of the second half of the eighteenth century. Their spread across much of provincial France was also closely intertwined with the growth of new cultural institutions in the provinces – provincial academies, reading rooms, masonic lodges, theatres. As was the case with English provincial papers, the *affiches* did show an interest in local history and local developments. This does not, however, seem to have signalled any challenge to values that were metropolitan in origin. As Claude Labrosse has noted, the *affiches* may have expounded the virtues of their province, but they portrayed them in 'relatively abstract terms' (Labrosse, 1983). Progress, more importantly, was defined in terms of norms established by the culture of Paris. As was the case in Britain, the structure of the press was an important factor reinforcing the national outlook of the *affiches*. Through the system of privileges operated by the French authorities, the *affiches* were kept firmly subordinate to the Paris press. 'The *Affiches*', Popkin has observed, 'were written in the national language, the scientific advances and the cultural innovations they disseminated came from Paris, and the journalistic niche they occupied was framed by privileges intended to fit them into a comprehensive journalistic system defined in national terms' (1993a, p. 438).

The movement towards the establishment of national cultural values and standards in this period should not be oversimplified. Integration, or attempted integration, did not signify passivity or simple suborbordination. Provincial cultures were not meekly submissive or uncritical of metropolitan culture (on this, see esp. Borsay, 1994). Neither did integration preclude the redefinition and increasing clarity of, in the Scottish case, national, and in the English and Welsh cases, provincial or regional identities. This can be shown very clearly by developments in Scotland.

As Colin Kidd has recently argued, at least as early as the later seventeenth century, models of constitutional, social and economic practice derived from English experience exercised a profound influence on Scottish opinion and debate (1993). In accepting or even adopting these models during the subsequent century, most Scots did not lose a sense of distinctive identity. There was, as one historian has put it, a 'dynamic of competitive emulation' at work after 1700 (Devine, 1983, p. 12). In the working out of new loyalties and identities within the context of increasingly uniform values and standards, the press had an important role to play. John Dwyer has even called it 'a critical mechanism for cultural unification' in Scotland (1989). This reflected a background of marked geographical and linguistic divisions, and poor transport and communications. The press, as Dwyer notes, served to link Scotland to 'modern European socioeconomic life'. It also represented an important forum for a debate about the distinctiveness of Scotland's position within this context and within Britain and the British empire. This debate focused on the values and standards that should be cultivated by Scotland's landowning classes – values and standards that were often defined in terms of hostility towards, or difference from, developments and trends in English society. This strand of debate gathered pace in the aftermath of the Seven Years War, when English, particularly metropolitan, opinion showed a virulent strain of anti-Scottish prejudice. Partly in reaction to this prejudice, many Scots sought to express a sense of cultural difference from England and English people. This took on political overtones in successive and overlapping agitations for a Scottish militia and parliamentary and burgh reform between the later 1750s and 1780s, agitations in which the press had an important role to play.

The relationship between emergent or changing identities and the adoption or emulation of metropolitan standards and values in an English context was obviously less problematic or politically sensitive than in Scotland. Yet, as John Money has shown in a detailed study of the evolution of Birmingham and the West Midlands, similar sorts of processes and concerns can be discerned (1977). Provincial papers, in the West Midlands and elsewhere, often gave expression to local pride at the same time as disseminating values and culture derived from the metropolis. As emphasized in an earlier chapter, this feature of newspaper content – pride in locality or, often, one's local town – and the developing regional and urban consciousness that underpinned it, can be very clearly discerned in the coverage of loyalist movements in 1745 and the 1790s. Reports of loyal activities or demonstrations usually sought to position local royalism in a national context. A Bristolian boasted in Felix Farley's *Bristol Journal* during the Jacobite Rebellion of 1745–6 that 'not a City in England is more firmly attach'd to his present Majesty's Person and Government than that of Bristol' (B. Harris, 1995b). Nearly fifty years later, between 1792 and 1793, large numbers of paragraphs declared the attachment of towns throughout Britain to George III and the constitution and their abhorrence of Thomas Paine, France and popular radicalism. On 10 June 1793, the local section of the *Reading Mercury and Oxford Gazette* was largely filled with paragraphs concerning the celebration of the King's birthday in towns in the locality. A sense of identity and local pride was being reinforced in terms of a contribution to, or identification with, a bigger, more inclusive, project or entity.

If newspapers played an important role in national integration at a cultural level, as well as in reflecting and reinforcing changing national and regional identities, they also promoted national integration at the political level. Again as emphasized elsewhere in this work, by its growing ability to open up Parliament to public scrutiny, the press helped to provide a common political vocabulary and framework within which the discussion of political developments and events could take place. The increasingly national incidence of the press also contributed to this sense of a common, national political discussion. Contemporaries were aware that contributions not just to London but also to Scottish and provincial papers could find a very widely dispersed audience. David Swinfen has pointed to the sense of inclusion in a debate encompassing not just Scotland but the whole of Britain revealed by contributors to the Scottish press during the American War (1976, p. 73):

> To some exent, the nature of the press itself helped to blur the lines of national demarcation. For its news of the American situation, the press in Scotland was heavily dependent on English sources.... Even the correspondence was to a large extent national – letters to the London press were frequently reprinted in Edinburgh, Glasgow and Aberdeen. *Many correspondents within Scotland made it clear that when they spoke of 'the nation' they meant the whole of the United Kingdom!*

(My emphasis)

The practice of many Scottish papers in the later eighteenth century of employing London correspondents can have only further strengthened the perception (an accurate one) that national political life was defined in terms of a series of relationships flowing from, and centred on, London.

Another way in which the press helped to foster identification with the nation, however defined, was through its reportage of foreign affairs and military events and actions. The social and economic forces and factors that shaped the scale of the public response to war and international rivalry in the eighteenth century were discussed in Chapter 1 and do not need rehearsing again here. Another very important factor was religion and, in particular, anti-Catholic sentiment. The fate of Protestants in Catholic Europe drew British eyes towards the continent (see Black, 1986; Colley, 1992; Haydon, 1993). International rivalry was often perceived and portrayed in religious terms, particularly before 1760. Frederick the Great, to give one prominent example, was projected during the Seven Years War in Britain as a popular Protestant hero; he was fighting to protect the Protestant religion in Germany. The press had a vital role to play in increasing awareness of international politics and rivalries. We saw in an earlier chapter the emphasis that all forms of the press placed on providing information and news about foreign affairs and the conditions of war and diplomacy. The sheer volume of information and news on foreign affairs that papers provided, particularly in periods of war or international tension, would be hard to exaggerate. News of military victories led to special editions of provincial papers, to provide their readers with the latest news. The few illustrations that appeared in eighteenth-century newspapers usually related to military events (on this, see esp. Cranfield, 1962, p. 269). The closeness with which many contemporaries followed reports of Britain's participation in war emerges very clearly from a number of sources. Diaries show consistent interest in military events. James Woodeforde, the Somerset parson and fellow of New College, Oxford, very rarely made entries about foreign affairs or domestic politics. When he did, however, they nearly always concerned major actions or events in war or international diplomacy. On 17 June 1780, he wrote: 'Charles Town taken and 8,000 of the Rebels killed and taken.' Three years later, on 25 January 1783, his diary records: 'This Evening the Ipswich News brought us the joyful News of Peace signed at Versailles the 20 of this month and reed [sic] at London the 25' (Beresford, 1926, vol. ii, p. 285; vol. iii, p. 57). The papers themselves also provide much evidence for the eagerness with which reports of expected military actions were received. The influential London tri-weekly paper, the *London Evening Post*, reported on 28 August 1758:

We hear from Bridport in Dorsetshire, that on the Rumour of our good success at Louisbourg, the inhabitants of that Place assembled in great Numbers, and sat up all night to wait for the Post-Boy, whom they met at the Entrance of the Town, and ushered in with Acclamations of Joy with the confirmation of their wishes.

Similar events and responses appear to have occurred on the same occasion throughout much of Britain.

Colley has argued that such incidents are powerful evidence of the swelling force of nationalism in Britain in the eighteenth century, a nationalism that cut across, and, by implication, weakened, class and social divisions (Colley, 1992). This is an arguable point. Much depends on definitions of nationalism and perceptions of its relationship to class identity (see the comments in Smout, 1989; Hobsbawm, 1990; Finn, 1993). There is no doubt, however, that the growth of the press ensured that Britain's participation in war had far-reaching ramifications at the level of perceptions and identities. A broad cross-section of society is likely, because of the press, to have developed a clearer sense of national identity and of their place in Britain's expanding empire. As part of this process, the press also helped to foster stronger attachment to symbols, often military in derivation, of national prowess. The most obvious of these, and the one that has attracted greatest attention, is the British navy (see Jordan and Rogers, 1989). Yet the growth in status of the army during this period is also a notable, if less often acknowledged, development. A good indication of the growing standing of the army is the use that local elites often made of it to project a positive image of the state and government, as the frequent use of the military in local celebrations of victories and loyal demonstrations shows. The enthusiasm for the militia in the later 1750s, highland regiments from around the same time, and for volunteering in the 1790s and early 1800s also reflected, in part, the attractions that were felt to surround military life, not least in respect of colourful and striking uniforms (see Colley, 1992; Gee, forthcoming).

All the developments discussed above had their centre of gravity among the upper and middling ranks. How far readership of the press served to challenge or redefine local identities and loyalties at levels in society much below the middling ranks is very difficult to say. It seems likely, however, that the answer is not much. Certainly in larger towns, the diversity of the inhabitants, the nature of urban life, relatively easy access to coffee houses, inns and shops, the existence of clubs and other forums for discussion and the exchange of views, all probably helped, together with ease of access to the press, to erode parochialism. Even in the larger towns, however, older identities and loyalties may have retained considerable force. Drawing on a contemporary diary, Mark Harrison has emphasized how a newcomer to Bristol in the early nineteenth century, which boasted a very sophisticated local political culture, found himself treated as a 'foreigner' (1988, pp. 200–1). What makes this example all the more striking is the fact that, as was common to most early modern migrants, the newcomer, a carpenter, was from a neighbouring county, in this case, Somerset.

The example of revolutionary France, where a far more concerted attempt than ever took place in contemporary Britain was made to implant national values and a sense of national identity – partly through sponsorship of papers – is perhaps also suggestive in this context. As Alan Forrest and Peter Jones have recently written (1991, p. 6): 'National unity... could be wafer thin, concealing a host of hatreds and disagreements. Repeated invocation of the French nation and the indivisibility of the Republic could not rid France of the images and mentalities of previous centuries...'

France displayed a much stronger sense of regionalism and localism in the eighteenth century than Britain. It was a much less integrated society, politically, economically and, at lower social levels, linguistically. But differences with Britain, in this context, should not be exaggerated. The extent of local disparities in Britain in terms of social structures, settlement patterns, forms of social control and levels of politicization is something that British political historians have tended not to examine very closely, partly because of problems of evidence. But these disparities undoubtedly did exist. We also know far more about political life and conditions in the larger towns and cities than in small market towns and rural villages (see the comments on this, and on regional and local diversity, in Black, 1993a). This is equally true in respect of the extent of readership of the press. There is some impressionistic evidence of newspapers being passed around among craftsmen and tradesmen, and among alehouse societies in small market towns and villages during the eighteenth century. There is also some evidence that radicals dispersed in villages in both England and Scotland were reading newspapers in the 1790s, and of the existence of often surprisingly extensive networks for distributing newspapers between groups in neighbouring areas or villages (O'Gorman, 1989, pp. 295–6; Logue, 1979, p. 103). How common this was, however, is very difficult to say. Joel Barlow claimed in 1792 that 'not one person in a hundred sees a newspaper once a year' (quoted in Smith, 1979, p. 151). Rab Houston has argued, with reference to Scotland and the northeast of England, that for most of the population, newspapers or print in any form probably did not replace oral forms of communication to any great degree (1985). Even if we can assume that elites or craftsmen in small market towns and villages did have access to newspapers, there is little evidence to suggest that local identities were weakened to any great extent in this period. 'Plebeian identity', as Fletcher and Stevenson have written, 'was rooted in the sense of belonging to a local environment.' Dialect, types of food and drink, and peculiar festivals and customs underpinned this strong identification with locality (1985, p. 9). John Cookson has recently discovered deep-rooted localism among the Sutton volunteers of Lincolnshire in the early 1800s (1991). Further research would almost certainly turn up more examples.

SOCIAL AND CULTURAL BOUNDARIES

The perception that the early modern period saw a widening gulf between popular and elite culture is a common one (see Burke, 1978; Thompson, 1991, esp. ch. 1). The growing influence and adoption of metropolitan standards and values is often portrayed as representing a significant deepening of this process (for this, see esp. Borsay, 1989). As sites of new leisure and cultural activities, towns, and the drift of the gentry towards them from the later seventeenth century, are held to symbolize the growing cultural and social divide. A study of Glamorganshire gentry has emphasized how they increasingly fell under the sway of metropolitan culture after 1660, partly through visiting Bath and the capital, and became increasingly distanced from native Welsh, predominantly oral, culture (Jenkins, 1983).

The growing use and presence of print in society has been portrayed as a further factor serving to increase the distance between elite and popular cultures (Eisenstein, 1986). It was increasingly through print that elite cultural values were disseminated after 1600. Yet the issue of whether the culture of print did, in fact, serve to harden social boundaries between the elite and the rest of society is a problematic one. Much of the debate on this area has concentrated on the relationship between literary and oral forms of communication. Critics of the view that print served to establish a firm division between a predominantly literate culture and a predominantly oral one emphasize the ways in which literary and oral forms interacted throughout the early modern period. Much print culture – for example, ballads and songs – drew on and exploited oral culture (Watt, 1991; Houston, 1985). As was emphasized in the Introduction to this book, oral forms of communication often ensured that audiences for printed information and news spread beyond the literate sections of society. The view, often expressed, that the literary forms common at different levels of society diverged from the seventeenth century also needs to be qualified. While chap-books, songs and ballads did have a disproportionate influence among a popular audience, it is far from being established that such forms of print culture were aimed exclusively at the lower ranks in society. Tessa Watt, looking at sixteenth- and early seventeenth-century England, has argued forcefully that ballads were probably read by both elite and non-elite groups in society (1991). Thomas Crawford has made a similar point about the role of song in Scotland in the eighteenth century (1979). As far as eighteenth-century England is concerned, the social composition of the audience for political ballads and songs is an underexplored topic. It seems, however, that certainly during the mid-eighteenth century, growing numbers of political ballads were written for dissemination primarily among the established political classes. Like much comment on domestic politics in early Hanoverian papers, the force of these ballads often relied on readers or hearers being able to understand complex allusions and possessing a close knowledge of political events and political personalities.

What difference the appearance and growth of newspapers made to the changing relationship between popular and elite cultures is very difficult to be precise about. In both Britain and France in this period newspapers do seem generally to have promoted a view of social and political development and change that stressed opposition or friction between an enlightened elite and an unenlightened populace. There was a perception among most contributors to newspapers that their readers did not share popular interests and superstitions. Jeremy Black has suggested that most English papers in the eighteenth century espoused views consistent with what is broadly termed the English Enlightenment – urbanity, tolerance, conviviality, moderation, humanitarianism (Black, 1987a, ch. 8). These values were often characterized by hostility towards, or suspicion of, popular habits and practices. This tendency to perceive society in terms of crude dualities was also reinforced by the impetus that social and economic change, and international rivalry, gave to a widespread will and desire for improvement and reform of the lower orders. This urge for reform found expression in projects such as workhouses, Sunday schools and hospitals, all of which were fully aired and discussed in the press (see esp. Andrew, 1989). Some papers positioned themselves in terms of their participation in an explicitly elitist culture. Henry Fielding's mid-century newspapers or journals – the *True Patriot*, the *Covent Garden Journal* – all sought to establish their learned credentials through, among other things, the liberal use of Latin and Greek quotations. Fielding implied or, at times, explicitly asserted that, by reading his papers, readers were segregating themselves from the mob. The relative complexity of the information and comment carried by most elements of the British press in the eighteenth century has been a major theme of earlier parts of this work. This may have added to the alienation or indifference that many lower down the social order probably felt towards the press.

Similar points can be made about the French and French-language press under the old regime. If anything, the gap between the French press and popular culture was even greater. This reflected in part the sober style and professionalism of the conductors of the French-language gazettes, but it also reflected tighter political control. The gazettes were journals of record. Their content rarely carried any sense of immediacy or political urgency. It was not designed to appeal to its readers at a directly emotional level. In this sense, they can be contrasted very clearly with the *libelles*, illegal, clandestine pamphlets which contained personalized scabrous, often pornographic attacks on leading French political figures, and which were disseminated widely in Paris from the mid-century. In their commentary and reporting, French journalists reflected their sense of membership of an intellectual and social elite. Jeremy Popkin has emphasized the elitist assumptions of Jean de Luzac, editor of the *Gazette de Leyde*. Popkin refers to Luzac's general coolness towards 'popular' movements that used force to achieve their goals (1989, p. 162). In this context, Luzac showed little liking for the exuberant political style of John Wilkes in Britain in the 1760s. The *affiches*, the cheapest of the French papers before 1789, and those most likely to reflect the views of France's expanding commercial and mercantile classes, also showed a strong sense of separation from the commonalty. J.R. Censer has recently detected a high degree of ambivalence in the social criticism of traditional elites in the *affiches*. He suggests that this reflected a perception by the writers that they formed part of an inclusive elite which embraced the older elites and which was united by its separation from the rest of society (1994, p. 77). Even after 1789, when journalism in France underwent a massive transformation, there were significant continuities with the press of the old regime. As Popkin has pointed out, Hébert's fictional Père Duchesne quoted Montaigne, while Desmoulins's *Révolutions de France et de Brabant* was 'virtually a course in Roman History' (1990, p. 45). No doubt, these papers were not read in an identical manner by all people. They were open to multiple interpretations. Yet genuinely popular literature in France in the eighteenth century was very different in character. The story of the Revolution was told in anonymous broadsides as well as in newspapers. These drew on imagery designed to make them comprehensible to ordinary citizens, to the semi-literate and illiterate as well as the literate (see Reichardt, 1989). Like songs and speeches, they were part of an 'ordinary world' of oral communication in a way that newspapers were not.

But a view of the early press that emphasizes its elitism can only be pushed so far. This is especially true of the early British press. A major problem is its sheer diversity. This was apparent in respect both of important differences between papers and in terms of differences between material carried in the same paper. Diversity was, in fact, a characteristic that most eighteenth-century British papers were seeking to achieve. The editor of a Jacobite paper of 1751–3, the *True Briton*, recognized the imperative of interspersing often dense discussion of political and religious matters with more entertaining fare. Whether he was successful in doing this is doubtful, since the paper's popularity declined rapidly in 1752 before it collapsed because of lack of readers and inadequate financial support early the following year (B. Harris, 1995c). In seeking to entertain, papers often exploited popular literary forms – songs, ballads, short verses. Some, particularly political, papers were very emotional in tone, and their content was far removed from the urbanity and moderation prized by the English Enlightenment. John Wilkes's *North Briton* stands out in this respect, with its deliberately populist style and exploitation of deeply rooted prejudices and anxieties. Wilkes had a number of emulators in the 1770s. His style of journalism had also surfaced earlier in the century in a variety of contexts and forms (see esp. Perry, 1962; Sack, 1993). In the 1770s and 1780s, the Reverend Henry Bate was responsible for making social scandal an important element in the London press (Werkmeister, 1963). The two papers with which Bate was associated at this time – the *Morning Herald* and the *Morning Post* – also displayed a strain of xenophobia, anti-semitism and hatred for Dissent that had surfaced periodically during the early Hanoverian period, but briefly disappeared in the later 1750s (Sack, 1993, p. 10). A recent critique of views of cultural development in England and Wales in this period which stress growing distance between the elites and the rest of the population is also relevant in this context. Jonathan Barry has suggested that such interpretations suffer from ambiguity about the role of the growing middling ranks in society and often ignore the way in which commercially minded innkeepers, most notably, sought to exploit the taste for new leisure pursuits quite far down the social scale (1985). The cultural values and standards that received their fullest expression among the propertied elite were very widely diffused, albeit in often amended forms. Notably broad social access to newspapers in the eighteenth century, particularly in the capital and larger towns, might be portrayed as another element of contemporary social realities that served to blur social distinctions, not define them more clearly. The language, the terms, that papers tended to use to describe society and social divisions may have actually helped this process. This is because in its ambiguity, its failure to specify in detail where the division between the enlightened elite and the rest fell, this language did not stand in the way of identification with ostensibly elite values by groups, for example, of skilled artisans and shopkeepers.

The relationship between newspapers and oral culture was also a complex one. This is more than simply a matter of newspapers being read out to illiterate or only partly illiterate audiences. Nicholas Rogers has argued in the context of a discussion of the intervention of crowd in early Hanoverian politics that it was because of the expansion of the press that urban festivals and demonstrations were renewed and transformed in the early eighteenth century. As Rogers remarks (1989, p. 353):

> Through the new medium of journalism, urban festival reached an expanding audience. With the changing urban prospect and the new dimensions of space, the carnivalesque lost its older territoriality and spread beyond the market place. The relationship of print to oral culture was not simply one of displacement. The new did not immediately supplant the old or render it vestigial.

The press did not report all popular demonstrations, not even all popular demonstrations on national political issues. In certain circumstances, it deliberately ignored them, usually where they were either seen as unduly threatening to social order or where a newspaper took opposite political sides to the demonstators. But by describing some of the larger, more notable popular political demonstrations in great detail, the press helped to popularize symbols and slogans that were deployed on the street. This process was, in fact, two-way. The crowd exploited symbols and motifs developed in the press as well as vice versa. By its use of the same symbols, the press helped to set demonstrations firmly in the context of national political struggles; the press gave many popular demonstrations a more than purely local significance. They were part of a political culture that was increasingly outward-looking. In the longer term, however, as we will see below (pp. 96–7), the press may have helped to drive a wedge between the politics of the street and the developing extraparliamentary politics of the propertied classes.

If the perception that the press helped to divide elite and popular culture, propertied and non-propertied groups in society, before 1800 needs, then, to be qualified in a number of important ways, how far was it a force in Britain before 1800 for a growing sense of collective identity among the expanding middling ranks or classes? The closeness of the relationship between the British press and the middling ranks in the eighteenth century has been emphasized in recent years by a number of historians (Schweizer and Klein, 1989, pp. 171–2; Stone and Stone, 1984, p. 418), and, in a superficial sense, the press did clearly have specifically 'middle-class' features. The bulk of its expanding readership, and certainly the growing numbers of newspaper purchasers, were, as argued in Chapter 1, probably accounted for by members of the middling ranks. This fact also shaped the varied content of the press, the emphasis on economic and commercial news, as well as on entertainment and political news and comment. The development of the press was also intimately related to the changes that principally benefited the middling ranks – economic progress, urbanization, expanding markets, etc. But once we go beyond this, the picture quickly becomes less clear. It is not certain, for example, that content analysis is particularly helpful or as straightforward as some historians have implied. Stephen Botein, Jack Censer and Harriet Ritvo have recently examined closely a number of features of press content among a group of British and French papers (1981). On the basis of their examination, they argue that, in comparison to the French press, British papers adopted a generally bourgeois tone and perspective. One feature of this supposed perspective on which they place considerable weight is the volume of criticism of the aristocracy in many papers. Many elements of the press, while serving to disseminate news and views of metropolitan fashion, also gave considerable space to items articulating a predominantly moral and cultural critique of fashionable London society and aristocratic patronage of foreign goods and services, which waxed most strongly in the 1750s, 1770s and 1780s (for this critique, see Newman, 1987). But was this critique peculiarly bourgeois in origin or appeal in an eighteenth-century context? Its appeal was not limited to middling groups in towns, and certainly embraced a large portion of the gentry, yeomen, tenant farmers and also certain members of the aristocracy. It is also possible to point to many items in papers which displayed or could be interpreted as displaying admiration for rank and in particular the titled nobility. Papers attached to spa towns and resorts often listed prominent visitors to these places. In this, the papers were exploiting the appeal of being seen in the same places as members of the aristocracy. Other papers often commented on paternalist gestures by members of the aristocracy, for example, the donation of money or food and clothing to the poor in periods of stress and hardship. Local celebrations of births and marriages in great families were often reported. In 1756, the *Newcastle Courant* praised and listed members of the northeast's social and political elites who had contributed to a fund to pay bounties to volunteers for the navy (10 April

1756). The range of material in the press makes it all too easy, in other words, to find support for contradictory views of the role and identity of the middling ranks in society. A lack of consensus among historians about how to portray the middling ranks in this period, as referred to earlier, only complicates matters further. Despite these problems, however, it does seem that in so far as the press did promote or reinforce social divisions, this may have been less a matter of promoting a distinctive sense of middle-class identity than, as already suggested, a matter of widening the gap between, on the one hand, the section of society that was literate and judicious, or those who accepted its values, and, on the other, the rest.

If it is difficult to portray the press as promoting, in cultural terms, a clearer sense of collective identity among the expanding middling ranks, how far might the press have done this through its political role and content? As we saw in an earlier chapter, the press certainly did have a creative role to play in increasing the reality and effectiveness of popular participation in politics. This participation, however, encompassed most groups among propertied society – landed gentry, farmers and the urban middling ranks – and extended beyond those sections of society that in the next century were to provide the core of a distinctive middle class. Paul Langford has argued that from around 1760 propertied society was seeking increasingly to distance itself from the crowd in political as well as social and cultural terms (1991, esp. pp. 466–75). In a Scottish context, Stana Nenadic has argued a similar case, although she portrays this as an important aspect of the formation of an increasingly distinctive middle class (1990). The factors that lay behind this were complex and various. In part, it reflected imperatives that stemmed from commercial and economic progress, in particular a sensitivity towards the desirability of good order and social stability. It was also in part a consequence of the reunification of landed society at the accession of George III, formerly divided into Whig and Tory parties. Before 1760, the Tories in particular were prepared to flirt with populist notions and strategies (Colley, 1981). The growing perception that popular disorder and riot was increasing in incidence from the later 1750s also fuelled a widespread concern about mechanisms of social control and their apparent weakening. The growth of the press, meanwhile, fuelled apprehension about popular politics. The press threatened to undermine the rule of property by opening up politics to the non-propertied. This anxiety was not new in the 1760s, but, with the strong growth of the press after 1760, and its increasing ability to circumvent political control, it was significantly heightened.

Paradoxically perhaps, while focusing many anxieties about social and economic change, the press may also have seemed to many to hold out the prospect of constructing a form of extraparliamentary politics that was relatively orderly and removed from the unruly forces of the street. Interestingly, the perception that the press and the street represented different orders of politics was expressed as early as 1742 by one Scottish MP (quoted in Black, 1990, p. 79):

> People here have been of late a little mobbish in different ways the better sort in sowing malicious clamour... we have sometimes little poetical satires and satirical pamphlets... from London.... The lower sort of people sometimes deal in mobbing properly so called.... The practice of mobbing ought to be stopped.

The press provided a forum for rational argument and persuasion, and for open forms of public politics. Petitioners emphasized their respectability. The *Leeds Mercury* emphasized that a Halifax petition in favour of conciliation with the colonies of late 1775 included, among its signatories, 'many Gentlemen of affluent fortunes, and as respectable characters as this county can boast' (14 November 1775). The Association movement also presented itself in the same terms, stressing the respectability and, often, the landed nature of its support. But perhaps the extraparliamentary campaigners that most successfully exploited the press in constructing a form of public pressure that managed, at least partially, to distance itself from overtones of political radicalism and any threat to stability were the anti-slave trade lobby. What is most striking about the movement for the abolition of the slave trade is how it survived in relatively unpromising political circumstances – the period of reaction and alarm created by the combination of popular radicalism and the threat from revolutionary France – and how rapidly and strongly it revived in the early 1800s (Drescher, 1994). How much this owed to astute presentation in and use of the press is a subject that deserves closer examination. Notices about meetings of those against the slave trade in the early 1790s tended to emphasize their cross-party and multi-denominational composition. Great stress was also laid on order and openness. By presenting their campaign in such terms, the abolition movement sought to distance itself from connotations of radicalism and challenge. The press was helping to construct a politics of respectability, a politics characterized by order and peaceful persuasion. Crucially, however, this was not, contra Nenadic, specifically a middle-class politics. Indeed, it appealed to sections of the landed elite as well as sections of the artisanal and shopkeeping classes. Many popular radicals in the 1790s were as convinced of the possibilities of effecting peaceful change through astute use of the press as middle-class reformers and humanitarians (on this, see Dinwiddy, 1990). The *Moral and Political*

Magazine of the London Corresponding Society, launched in mid-1796, declared that its aim was 'to form a pure channel of instruction to the peasant, the artificer and the labourer: of instruction, as well concerning the natural and proper duties and rights of men in general, as respecting the temporary posture of their public concerns'. Respectability was a cultural force that cut across social and economic divisions; it was the preserve of no single group or rank in society.

THE IDEA OF A FREE PRESS

If development of the press cannot easily be seen as having helped to crystallize a distinctive middle-class identity in eighteenth-century Britain, the press did nevertheless expand political and cultural horizons; it opened up politics and culture to an ever broader cross-section of society. It did this at the level of ideology, as well as in practical ways. In both Britain and France, the press helped to inspire new ways of thinking about culture and politics, new ways of conceptualizing cultural and political authority. One of the principal ways in which it did this was by focusing attention on the concept and value of a free press.

This is an aspect of the intervention of the press in politics that requires further enquiry. A number of historians have looked at various aspects of this topic for Britain, although not all periods have been equally well covered (see esp. Gunn, 1983; Hellmuth, 1990). For France, relevant work is very slight indeed, although interesting avenues of enquiry have been opened up (Baker, 1989; Furet and Ozouf, 1989; Van Kley, 1994; Goodman, 1994).

In Britain, attitudes towards press freedom were very closely shaped by the logic of parliamentary politics. The notion that a free press was an essential bulwark of liberty became important in public discussion from at least the 1730s (Gunn, 1983, pp. 88–9). This development reflected in part the need for opposition politicians to find new ways of bringing popular pressure to bear on Parliament following the passage of the Septennial Act (1716) and the establishment of Whig oligarchy (after 1722 opposition politicians could no longer expect to topple ministers at elections). The use of the press by opposition politicians, symbolized by the involvement of leading opposition politicians William Pulteney and Lord Bolingbroke with the weekly essay paper the *Craftsman* (founded in 1726), also encouraged discussion in the press of the role of popular opinion in politics. At various times during the early Hanoverian period the opposition press sought to present public opinion as an important actor in politics and to defend the right of the public to examine political questions and make their views known on the major issues of the day. In this context, far-reaching claims were made on occasion regarding the social inclusiveness of the political nation (see esp. Wilson, 1992). The press thus served as a progressive and creative force in contemporary ideological debate.

Public discussion of the role of the press and public opinion continued to be shaped by the course of parliamentary politics in the later eighteenth century. Supporters of both the ministry and opposition, inside and outside Parliament, continued to express their support for press freedom. Ministerial supporters, however, were more prone, like their counterparts earlier in the century, to warn about the dangers of 'license' in the press and about abuses of press freedom and the threat that this posed to political liberty and social order. The opposition, meanwhile, particularly growing numbers of extra-parliamentary radicals and reformers, saw in the press ways of reinforcing arguments about public accountability and public participation in politics. Serious differences also persisted regarding the composition and identity of the political nation, with ministers favouring a more socially exclusive definition. Yet at the same time, under the impact of political events such as the constitutional crisis of 1782–4, ministers and their supporters, like their opposition counterparts, did come to accept that public opinion was and should be an important factor in political life. This secular shift in attitudes towards the press and public opinion was almost certainly a factor in the relative circumspection shown by the government in its dealings with newspapers during the fraught decade of the 1790s. As already mentioned, major new legislative restrictions on the press were eschewed by Pitt the Younger and his ministers. The importance of the shift in attitudes is well illustrated by the passage of Charles James Fox's Libel Act in 1792. This act finally settled long-standing arguments about the proper province of the jury in libel trials in favour of the jury (see esp. Green, 1985, pp. 318–55). Although we lack a full legislative history of the Act, the parliamentary debates indicate no or at least negligible opposition to the principle of the bill. Indeed, the ministry and its legal officers seem to have supported the objectives of the measure; the only modifications they insisted on concerned procedure and technical legal points. Throughout the eighteenth century, steady, cumulative pressure built up in favour of the rights of the press and of free speech. This was one aspect of a broader liberalization of political life in Britain after 1760.

In France, the press, and the concept of a free press, also furnished individuals with an important basis for reconceptualizing the nature of political authority. Yet political conditions were very different in France – there was, for example, no comparable tradition or practice of parliamentary politics. Partly because of this, and because of tighter political control, the periodical press itself did not play a direct role in discussions about liberty and press freedom. In so far as it did make a contribution in this sphere, it was necessarily indirect. Not even the gazettes published beyond France's borders ever sought to dramatize public opinion as a force in politics, or to engage in a debate about reshaping the nature of political life in France; their political messages were implicit. As Popkin succinctly remarks (Popkin, 1989, p. 136): 'In reading the *Gazette de Leyde*, ordinary subscribers were simultaneously admitted to the realm of public affairs and yet reminded of their powerlessness to affect it.'

If, therefore, we wish to find the locus of this debate, we need to look elsewhere. One important suggestion in this context has been recently made by Dena Goodman (1994). Goodman argues that a crucial influence on the debate about the role of the press and its relationship to liberty in France before 1789 was the French Enlightenment, the attempt of Enlightenment thinkers to transform French society 'in the image of the Republic of Letters'. This project chose as its first and principal terrain of engagement literary and philosophical matters. Its goal was knowledge, the truth. This was to be achieved through polite discussion, order, harmony and sociability. Arbiter of the truth was to be public opinion, but by this was meant not the opinion of the people but true judgement. This judgement was itself the product of 'enlightenment'; it was also viewed as being objective and universal.

Ideas and concepts articulated in cultural and philosophical debate in France were increasingly applied to politics in the later eighteenth century. Public opinion, for example, was increasingly invoked as a source, by many as the ultimate source, of political authority. Yet it was the public opinion of enlightened thinkers, not the public opinion that arises out of the heterogeneous and diverse interests and ideas in society. What may also have recommended this particular notion of public opinion to many French political thinkers was the fact that it fitted neatly with the emphasis among opponents of monarchical absolutism on the sovereignty of the nation seen as a single entity (for contemporary notions of 'nation' and 'sovereignty', see Baker, 1989).

Keith Baker has suggested that the emerging notion of public opinion in France in the later eighteenth century displayed many of the ambiguities later shown by the notion of the revolutionary will that was to supersede it. In this way, he is seeking (following in the footsteps of François Furet) to emphasize what he sees as important continuities between the political culture of the old regime and revolutionary politics. He is looking forward in particular to the bloody search for unanimity and ideological purity during the Terror of 1793–4. Seen as essentially single, the notion of public opinion was easily elided with the notion of public spirit, which encapsulated for the revolutionary cadres the ideal of political unanimity. Yet, Baker's is perhaps too neat a conceptualization of the progress and dynamics of ideological debate in France before and after 1789. It underplays the messy reality of political debate in France in this period. An indication of the range of political views articulated in France prior to the Revolution has recently been provided by Dale Van Kley in an examination of the wave of political pamphleteering that accompanied the pre-revolutionary crisis of 1787–9 (1994). Significantly in this present context, important elements of this debate were politicized notions of public opinion and of a free press.

The ambivalence and messiness that often characterized ideological debate in France in this period are also captured, as historians are increasingly emphasizing, in the founding document of the Revolution – 'The Declaration of the Rights of Man and of the Citizen' (for this, and the Declaration in general, see Van Kley, 1994). This contained clauses that protected the individual against the state, as well as including clauses that were focused on the rights to equality. Among the former was a guarantee of a free press. This reflected a strong confidence in France after 1789 in a free press, which was to last until 1791. Laws to govern press offences were proposed in 1790 and in 1791, but these were vigorously resisted, and while the proposals of 1791 were included in the constitution of that year, they were never enforced (Furet and Ozouf, 1989, p. 775). Genuine press freedom was fleeting, however, as the deaths of a significant number of journalists during the Terror signalize. Yet a moderated form of press freedom did re-emerge following the return in France to moderate constitutionalism in 1795 before disappearing again with the rise of the Bonapartiste dictatorship in 1799. This perhaps shows, as does the subsequent course of politics in the nineteenth century, that the value placed in France on a free press as an essential support for political liberty was only temporarily and partially defeated by the terroristic campaigns of the Jacobin radicals of 1793–4.

CONCLUSIONS

The press had significant effects on contemporary perceptions of social, political and cultural realities. In general terms, the press was a powerful vehicle for national integration, at a cultural and political level. The press also helped to reinforce changes in perceptions of locality, of region or, in a Scottish case, nation. It encouraged their definition in terms that derived from national or metropolitan debate. How far down the social scale its influence descended in this context is very difficult to say, but it certainly encompassed the bulk of upper and middling ranks.

The press also helped to shape and strengthen perceptions of a common British identity in this period. This was partly through popularizing a series of symbols of national achievement and vitality – overseas trade, the colonies, empire, the navy, the army. Through its remarkably full coverage of international politics, the press also under-lined the reality of international rivalry and Britain's changing but distinctive diplomatic and international role during the eighteenth century. In so doing, it helped to give individuals a better sense of their own place in Britain's empire, as well as of the extent and reach of Britain's global power.

Whether the press served before 1800 to distinguish the middling ranks in Britain from other groups in society, and provide them with a greater sense of collective identity, is very doubtful. It might as well be argued that the press encouraged these groups to identify with those above them on the social scale. In their anxiety to portray the eighteenth-century press as 'middle class', some historians have perhaps been too influenced by hindsight. In the early nineteenth century, groups that did seek to establish a distinctive middle-class identity used the press to further this aim (see esp. Cookson, 1982). The structure of the British press also began to change quite fundamentally. Papers became more highly capitalized. They established a firmer business identity. The press also developed an increasingly distinctive *collective* identity, partly based on perceptions of new found political importance and independence. This change was symbolized by the emergence of the notion of 'the fourth estate' (Gunn, 1983, pp. 88–92). As we have seen, tendencies in this direction were present in the eighteenth century – for example, in terms of developing ideas about the importance of the press in the political sphere – but they were embyronic. If the press had a wider contribution to make to social and class formation in the eighteenth century, it was probably to reinforce the cohesion of propertied society, to emphasize areas and values on which different groups within that section of society could agree and around which they could organize themselves. This cohesion did not, however, preclude or impede the development of serious political divisions, as the development of an increasingly partisan press in the later eighteenth century very clearly shows.

Finally, in both Britain and France the press played an important role in helping individuals and groups to conceptualize cultural and political authority in new ways. There was an element of cross-fertilization in this regard. John Wilkes and Jean Baptiste-Antoine Suard, for example, corresponded about the role of the press in politics in both countries (see Baker, 1989, pp. 197–8; Goodman, 1994, pp. 160–1). Yet, as so often, it is the dissimilarities that seem to stand out, although much more work could profitably be done on this topic. Views of press freedom and of public opinion in Britain were powerfully shaped by the changing conditions of politics, by the ways in which politicians and printers sought to use the press to intervene in politics. In France, the same debate, and the discursive practices and forms that shaped it, were most fully developed in non-political spheres. The politicization of French debate was a complex and discontinuous process; it was associated with periods of political crisis. There was also, perhaps because of these factors, less acceptance of dissidence, of pluralism. Public opinion was envisaged as single, as outside the messy commerce of politics.

Conclusion

One of the starting points for this book was Jürgen Habermas's theory of the public sphere. In recent years, there have been many criticisms of this theory. A crucial element is the notion that the eighteenth century marked a distinctive phase in the history of capitalism, a phase marked by dispersed economic power. It was the diffusion of control over wealth and the means of wealth creation that underpinned the emergence of a new political space that was shaped by predominantly bourgeois individuals operating as individuals. When Habermas was writing, in the 1960s, economic reductionism such as this was widely accepted. Today, following the collapse of Communist regimes in many parts of the globe, and the concomitant decline in the influence of Marxist theories in the social sciences and history, it is in full retreat. The notion of the eighteenth century marking a distinctive phase of capitalism is, in any case, itself extremely difficult to defend. Capitalist relationships and commercialization have historically very deep roots in English and French society. English society was already significantly commercialized by 1700.

But for all the criticisms, Habermas's perception that the eighteenth century did see fundamental changes in political culture, particularly in respect of its public dimension, remains a valuable one. In both Britain and France, from the later seventeenth century, new bodies and organizations, new forms of sociability, as well as new, more pervasive and faster means of communication, did come into being to give more visible form and force to public opinion, or at least different strands of this public opinion. There was also undoubtedly a very close relationship between these developments and social and economic change, even if its meaning and significance were somewhat different to how Habermas represented these.

The growth of the press, which Habermas called the 'pre-eminent institution' of his public sphere, was, as we have seen, very closely shaped by social and economic change. The development of the press was, in one sense, parasitic on broad-based economic progress, growing wealth among the middling ranks in society, expanding markets, improving communications and a trend, more marked in Britain than in France, for an increasing proportion of the population to live in towns. Towns, in fact, were absolutely crucial to the development of the early press. Both in terms of production and identity, the press was intimately bound up with urban society and economy. It required towns to be of a certain size before a printer could contemplate establishing a business in one of them. In Britain before the later eighteenth century, provincial printers founded newspapers not because they were profitable but because they formed a useful adjunct to their business. When provincial papers did become profitable, towards the end of the eighteenth century, it was owing to rising demand for advertising space from urban tradesmen and providers of services or leisure. Towns were also vital agents in the diffusion of newspapers. Towns provided much greater access to papers than rural locations, whether through coffee houses, inns and shops, or by more informal means. It was also largely owing to developing economic and physical links between towns and between towns and the countryside that newspapers were dispersed in rural areas or that rural-dwellers or inhabitants of small villages and market towns gained some access to the press. Seen from this perspective, the press is one of a number of factors in this period that were redefining in important ways the frontier between urban and rural society, as well as perceptions of this frontier.

How far, *qua* Habermas, was the press the crucial instrument of the new political spaces that were opening up in the eighteenth century? For many (perhaps a majority) of contemporaries, the association between the press and change seemed obvious. A sense of novelty, of new and different political horizons, was often powerfully expressed by contemporaries and by the press itself. Historians have found it difficult not to become very influenced by the force of these judgements. Yet one thing of which it is very important not to lose sight is the fact that before the advent of the press, the population was far from completely lacking means or the capacity to discuss political events. In fact, as this book has sought to emphasize at various points, private communication, rumour, word of mouth, the pulpit, and other forms of printed and hand-written propaganda (posters, handbills, etc.) all continued to constitute vital means of political communication *after* the rise of the press. The press, in many ways, supplemented and extended the effects of these forms of communication; it did not completely replace them.

Nevertheless, in Britain throughout the period 1620–1800 and in

France, especially after 1789, the press did grow in importance as a means of political communication. This reflected distinctive qualities which it possessed as means of disseminating information and ideas. As Jeremy Popkin has emphasized, unlike other aspects of contemporary print culture, it held out the possibility of continuous communication, of amplification and correction (1987). It established continuous circuits of communication, linking reader to paper, and reader to reader. In Britain, after 1771, the press was capable of offering an unfolding narrative of national political events. The press also came to be, albeit at different times in Britain and France, for most of its readers, an unparalleled source of information about domestic and foreign politics. It offered far more complete coverage of politics, domestic and foreign, than most individuals' personal contacts could be expected to furnish.

The repercussions of the growth of the press for the texture and nature of political life and culture is an area that still requires further research. Despite a continuously strengthening interest in the history of the early press in the last few decades, and in particular in its political role and importance, large gaps in our knowledge of these things remain. The absence of major modern studies of the later eighteenth-century provincial press in England and Wales (although see Barker, 1994) and the early Scottish press are among the most obvious. There has also been little detailed reseach into the use of the press by commercial and manufacturing lobbies, particularly in the 1780s and beyond. Yet it is unlikely that such work, if and when it is done, would overturn a number of important conclusions that emerge from existing studies. The first of these is that it was in Britain that these repercussions were first and most strongly felt. Recent attempts to demonstrate the supposed liveliness and importance of the French press under the old regime have undoubtedly done much to illuminate a neglected aspect of French politics in this period, but they do not support the view that the differences between the French and British press have been overemphasized in the past. Whether viewed in terms of circulation, readership, censorship or interventions in political life, the British press was a hugely more significant and independent actor in politics, as well as in social and cultural discussion and debate. This disparity is a factor that has not been sufficiently emphasized in recent debates about whether Britain in the eighteenth century was an overwhelmingly aristocratic society, a confessional state, and broadly similar to those in Europe. Viewed through the prism of the press, the political cultures of Britain and France, at least before 1789, appear to have been very different indeed.

In Britain, particularly after 1695, the growth of a politically active and influential press helped to produce a political culture that became more and more oriented around national political issues and divisions. The press ensured that partisanship in the centre was refracted throughout a growing cross-section of society. It helped to provide a common framework and vocabulary for public political debate. The press also helped to create new, and redefine older, perceptions of nation, region and locality. Political culture also became more open. Politicians became increasingly aware of the public nature of their activities. Their utterances took on a new significance because of this. They were aware of speaking, very often, to different audiences simultaneously, one inside and a growing one outside Parliament. The nature of the audience 'without doors' was also changed in more creative ways by the press. The press became the vehicle for new forms of public politics. The emergence of the petition as a major feature of political agitations in Britain in the later eighteenth century symbolizes this development. At every stage of petitioning – campaigning for meetings to draw them up, publicizing these meetings, publicizing the results of these meetings and the ensuing petitions, responding to their reception by Parliament – the press was fully involved.

An emphasis on change is therefore entirely appropriate when discussing the early press. Yet it is important to put the growth of the early press into some sort of wider social perspective. In both Britain and France before 1800, the press probably only touched the lives of a minority of people. The French Revolution may have led to the creation of a press on a scale never before seen in western Europe, even in Britain, yet it left vast areas of society unaffected. This was a reflection of the heavily agrarian nature of both societies, particularly so in the case of France. The press, before 1800, made little impression among the majority of the rural population, partly because of low levels of literacy. But literacy, or rather illiteracy, form only part of the explanation. Even among the urban population, where levels of literacy were on the whole higher, it is likely that readership of the press was confined to the skilled working classes, to artisans and craftsmen. In fact, the eighteenth-century press appears to have made little effort to court potential readers at social levels below this, although this is another area that requires much more detailed research. In terms of content and outlook, most papers sought to identify themselves with elite culture. And while the homogeneity of this culture is easily exaggerated, most strands of it do seem to have shared a hostility towards the mob, towards popular superstition, habits and culture. Most papers, especially in the eighteenth century, eschewed the sensationalism, the escapism, the interest in magic and prophecy, which were the principal characteristics of popular literature in this period. Even during the French Revolution, what is perhaps striking about the French press is how limited the attempts were that were made to adopt genuinely popular rhetorical styles and language by ostensibly 'popular' journalists. Radicals like Camille Desmoulins and Maximilien Robespierre were steeped in classical culture. Some of their journalism, particularly Robespierre's, was undoubtedly very extreme and very violent, but it did not discard that inheritance (on this, see Chisick, 1991b, p. 9).

The vast majority of purchasers, as well as readers, of newspapers appear to have come from the middling and upper ranks of society. It was the expansion of the middling ranks, and their growing wealth that lay behind the growth of the press in Britain throughout the period covered in this book and in France particularly from the mid-eighteenth century. They had the income, interest and incentive to subscribe regularly to newspapers. This is not to overlook the importance of newspaper readership higher up the social ranks. Politicians, like Edmund Burke, liked to claim to disregard the press, but they were, in reality, some of the most avid consumers of its contents, hence perhaps their often touchy sensitivity towards adverse comments about them in it. (Burke's disdain towards the press, it is perhaps also worth noting, did not go so far as omitting to furnish it with polished versions of his parliamentary speeches.) It was, nevertheless, the growing middling ranks, and their varied interests and concerns, that increasingly shaped the contents of most papers.

The extent to which, because of this, the press transformed social and cultural identities in this period is an aspect of the early press for which the evidence is most opaque and difficult to interpret. Much more work needs to be done on the social and moral contents of the press, preferably of a comparative nature, before we will reach any firm conclusions in this context. The press does, however, seem to have been a powerful force for the diffusion of common, metropolitan standards and values among the propertied parts of society. In doing this, it almost certainly served to widen or reinforce a gap that was already opening up in this period between the propertied and non-propertied. How far it also led, in Britain at least, to an increasing sense of collective importance and identity among its fastest-growing group of readers, the middling ranks, is very difficult to discern. The press was certainly seen at the time as threatening traditional political relationships, and the supremacy of landed influence and landed values in politics. This perception was not without justification. The press did lend itself to a politics founded upon argument and persuasion, as opposed to one principally on influence and interest. To this extent, the press can be seen to have helped the middling ranks develop a clearer sense of inclusion in national political culture. Yet at the same time, it reflected and reinforced divisions and diversity among the propertied ranks in society. It also provided a vehicle through which the traditional political classes could renew their hold on political power and revitalize their appeal. In Britain, some papers may have given expression to radical critiques of society and the political system, but others mounted concerted defences of these things. It is vital always to bear in mind, in this context, the nature of the press before 1800. It was still in a formative phase; it had yet to develop a separate or distinctive identity. Because of this, it acted as a fairly accurate mirror to the fissures, contradictions and ambivalences that ran through particularly propertied society in this period. Dror Wahrman has recently argued that there was a profound cultural rift in English society in the eighteenth century, between those sections of the propertied classes who identified themselves with what he has called 'national society', defined largely in terms of metropolitan values and standards, and 'communal-provincial society', which was defined largely in terms of a focus on the local community and in opposition to the former (Wahrman, 1992a). The usefulness of portraying society in this period in terms of such stark alternatives is debatable. But more important in the present context is the fact that Wahrman recognizes that the press 'could serve not only the national society but also the opposition to it'. In short, the social messages and meanings carried by the British press, certainly before 1800, were complex and diverse.

Bibliography

This bibliography includes all works referred to in the text of this book, as well as other major works on the French and British press between 1620 and 1800. All articles and books are published in London unless otherwise indicated.

FRANCE

Acomb (1973): Frances Acomb, *Mallet du Pan (1749–1800): A Career in Political Journalism* (Durham, N.C.).

Albaric (1980): Michel Albaric, 'Un page d'histoire de la presse clandestine: "Les Nouvelles ecclésiastiques", 1728–1803,' *Revue française d'histoire du livre*, 10: 319–32.

Albertan and Albertan (1989): Christian and Sylvianne Albertan, 'Les Silences de la presse provinciale en 1788', in Rétat (1989), pp. 25–35.

Ascoli (1977): Peter Ascoli, 'The French Press and the American Revolution: The Battle of Saratoga', *Proceedings of the 5th Annual Meeting of the Western Society for French History*, pp. 46–55.

Baker (1987): Keith Michael Baker, 'Politics and Public Opinion under the Old Regime: Some Reflections', in Censer and Popkin (1987), pp. 204–46.

Baker (1989): Keith Michael Baker, *Inventing the French Revolution: Essays on French Political Culture in the Eighteenth Century* (Cambridge).

Bellanger *et al.* (1969): *Histoire générale de la presse française*, vol. 1: *Des Origines à 1814* (Paris).

Benhamou (1992): Paul Benhamou, 'Inventaire des instruments de lecture publique de gazettes', in Duranton, Labrosse and Rétat (1992), pp. 121–9.

Botein, Censer and Ritvo (1981): Stephen Botein, Jack R. Censer and Harriet Ritvo, 'The Periodical Press in Eighteenth Century English and French Society: A Cross-Cultural Approach', *Comparative Studies in Society and History*, 23: 464–90.

Bots (1988): Hans Bots (ed.) *La Diffusion et la lecture des journaux de la langue française sous l'ancien régime* (Amsterdam).

Censer (1976): J.R. Censer, *Prelude to Power: The Parisian Radical Press, 1789–91* (Baltimore).

Censer (1987): J.R. Censer, 'English Politics in the *Courrier d'Avignon*', in J.R.

Censer and J.D. Popkin (eds), *Press and Politics in Pre-Revolutionary France* (Berkeley), pp. 71–7.

Censer (1994): J.R. Censer, *The French Press in the Age of Enlightenment.*

Censer and Popkin (1987): 'Historians and the Press', in J.R. Censer and J.D. Popkin (eds) *Press and Politics in Pre-Revolutionary France* (Berkeley), pp. 1–23.

Chartier (1989): Roger Chartier (ed.) *The Culture of Print: Power and the Uses of Print in Early Modern Europe*, trans. Lydia Cochrane (Princeton).

Chartier (1991): Roger Chartier, *The Cultural Origins of the French Revolution* (Durham, N.C.).

Chisick (1991a): Harvey Chisick, 'Politics and Journalism in the French Revolution: The Readership of the *Journal de la Montagne* and the Jacobin Clubs', *French History*, 5: 345–72.

Chisick (1991b): Harvey Chisick (ed.) *The Press in the French Revolution*, papers prepared for the conference 'Presse d'élite, presse populaire et propagande pendant la Révolution française' held at the University of Haifa, 16–18 May 1988 under the auspices of the Institut d'Histoire et de la Civilisation Françaises, *Studies on Voltaire*, vol. 287 (Oxford).

Chisick (1992): Harvey Chisick, *The Production, Distribution and Readership of a Conservative Journal of the Early French Revolution: The Ami du Roi of the Abbé Royou* (Philadelphia).

Darnton (1982): Robert Darnton, *The Literary Underground of the Old Regime* (Cambridge, Mass.).

Darnton and Roche (1989): Robert Darnton and Daniel Roche (eds) *Revolution in Print: The Press in France 1775–1800.*

Doyle (1989): William Doyle, *Origins of the French Revolution* (Oxford, 2nd edn).

Duranton, Labrosse and Rétat (1992): Henri Duranton, Claude Labrosse and Pierre Rétat (eds) *Les Gazettes européennes de langue française (XVIIe–XVIIIe siècles)* (St Etienne).

Edelstein (1977): Melvin Edelstein, *La Feuille villageoise: communication et modernisation dans les régions rurales pendant la Révolution* (Paris).

Eisenstein (1979): Elizabeth L. Eisenstein, *The Printing Press as an Agent of Change*, 2 vols (Cambridge).

Eisenstein (1986): Elizabeth L. Eisenstein, 'On Revolution and the Printed Word', in Roy Porter and Mikulas Teich (eds) *Revolution and History* (Cambridge), pp. 186–205.

Eisenstein (1991): Elizabeth L. Eisenstein, 'The Tribune of the People: A New Species of Demagogue', in Chisick (1991b), pp. 145–59.

Eisenstein (1992): Elizabeth L. Eisenstein, *Grub Street Abroad: Aspects of the French Cosmopolitan Press from the Age of Louis XIV to the French Revolution* (Oxford).

Fajn (1972): Max Fajn, 'The Circulation of the French Press during the French Revolution', *English Historical Review*, 87: 100–5.

Farge (1994): Arlette Farge, *Subversive Words: Public Opinion in Eighteenth-Century France*, trans. Rosemary Morris (Oxford).

Feyel (1982): Gilles Feyel, *La 'Gazette' en Province à travers ses réimpressions, 1631–1752* (Amsterdam).

Feyel (1984): Gilles Feyel, 'La Presse provinciale au XVIIIe siècle: géographie d'un réseau', *Revue historique*, cclxxii: 353–74.

Feyel (1988): Gilles Feyel, 'La Gazette au début de la guerre de sept ans: son administration, sa diffusion (1751–1758)', in Bots (1988), pp. 101–16.

Feyel (1992): Gilles Feyel, 'La Diffusion des gazettes étrangères en France et la révolution postale des années 1750', in Duranton, Labrosse and Rétat (1992), pp. 81–98.

Forrest and Jones (1991): Alan Forrest and Peter Jones (eds) *Reshaping France: Town, Country and Region during the French Revolution* (Manchester).

Furet and Ozouf (1989): François Furet and Mona Ozouf (eds) *A Critical Dictionary of the French Revolution* (Cambridge, Mass.).

Gelbart (1987): Nina Gelbart, *Feminine and Opposition Journalism in Old Regime France* (Berkeley).

Gilchrist and Murray (1971): J. Gilchrist and W.J. Murray, *The Press and the French Revolution* (New York).

Goodman (1994): Dena Goodman, *The Republic of Letters: A Cultural History of the French Enlightenment* (Ithaca and London).

Gough (1988): Hugh Gough, *The Newspaper Press in the French Revolution*.

Gough (1991): Hugh Gough, 'The Provincial Press in the French Revolution', in Forrest and Jones (1991), pp. 193–205.

Habermas (1989): Jürgen Habermas, *The Structural Transformation of the Public Sphere: An Inquiry into a Category of Bourgeois Society*, trans. Thomas Burger (Cambridge, Mass.).

Hatin (1859–61): Eugène Hatin, *Histoire politique et littéraire de la presse en France*, 8 vols (Paris).

Hatin (1865): Eugène Hatin, *Les Gazettes de Hollande et la presse clandestine aux XVIIe et XVIIIe siècles* (Paris).

Hunt (1984): Lynn Avery Hunt, *Politics, Culture and Class in the French Revolution* (Berkeley and Los Angeles).

Jones (1991): Colin Jones, 'Bourgeois Revolution Revivified: 1789 and Social Change', in Colin Lucas (ed.) *Rewriting the French Revolution* (Oxford), pp. 69–118.

Joynes (1987): Caroll Joynes, 'The *Gazette de Leyde*: The Opposition Press and French Politics, 1750–1757', in J.R. Censer and J.D. Popkin (eds) *Press and Politics in Pre-Revolutionary France* (Berkeley), pp. 133–69.

Kaplan (1976): Stephen L. Kaplan, *Bread, Politics and Political Economy in the Reign of Louis XV*, 2 vols (The Hague).

Kaplan (1984): Stephen L. Kaplan, *The Damiens Affair and the Unravelling of the Ancien Regime, 1750–1770* (Princeton).

Kennedy (1982): Michael L. Kennedy, *The Jacobin Clubs in the French Revolution: The First Years* (Princeton).

Kennedy (1984): Michael L. Kennedy, 'The Jacobin Clubs and the Press: "Phase Two"', *French Historical Studies*, 13: 474–99.

Klaits (1976): Joseph Klaits, *Printed Propaganda under Louis XIV* (Princeton).

Labrosse (1983): Claude Labrosse, 'La Région dans la presse régionale', in Jean Sgard (1983).

Labrosse and Rétat (1985): Claude Labrosse and Pierre Rétat, *L'Instrument périodique: la fonction de la presse au XVIIIe siècle* (Lyons).

Labrosse and Rétat (1989): Claude Labrosse and Pierre Rétat, *Naissance du journal révolutionnaire* (Lyons).

Levy (1980): Darline Grey Levy, *The Ideas and Careers of Simon-Nicolas-Henri Linguet: A Study in Eighteenth-Century French Politics* (Urbana).

Lojek (1977): Jerzy Lojek, 'Gazettes internationales de langue française dans le seconde moitié du XVIIIe siècle', in *Modèles et moyens de la réflexion politique au XVIIIe siècle*, 3 vols (Lille), vol. i, pp. 369–82.

McCleod (1989): Jane McCleod, 'A Bookseller in Revolutionary Bordeaux', *French Historical Studies*, 16: 262–83.

Mornet (1967): Daniel Mornet, *Les Origines intellectuelles de la Révolution française, 1715–1787* (Paris).

Moulinas (1974): René Moulinas, *L'Imprimerie, la librairie et la presse à Avignon au XVIIIe siècle* (Grenoble).

Murray (1986): William James Murray, *The Right-Wing Press in the French Revolution: 1789–92*.

Nathans (1990): Benjamin Nathans, 'Habermas's "Public Sphere" in the Era of the French Revolution', *French Historical Studies*, 16: 620–44.

Peyraud (1989): Christine Peyraud, 'Le Journalisme politique dans l'ouest en révolution', *History of European Ideas*, 10: 455–69.

Popkin (1980): Jeremy D. Popkin, *The Right-wing Press in France, 1792–1800* (Chapel Hill).

Popkin (1984): Jeremy D. Popkin, 'The Book Trades in Western Europe during the Revolutionary Era', *Papers of the Bibliographical Society of America*, 78: 403–45.

Popkin (1987): Jeremy D. Popkin, 'The Pre-Revolutionary Origins of Political Journalism', in Keith Michael Baker, François Furet and Colin Lucas (eds) *The French Revolution and the Creation of Modern Political Culture*, vol. I, ed. Keith Michael Baker, *The Political Culture of the Old Regime* (Oxford), pp. 203–23.

Popkin (1988): Jeremy D. Popkin, 'Un Journaliste face au marché des périodiques à la fin du dix-huitieme siècle: Linguet et ses *Annales* de Linguet', in Bots (1988), pp. 11–19.

Popkin (1989): Jeremy D. Popkin, *News and Politics in the Age of Revolution: Jean Luzac's 'Gazette de Leyde'* (Ithaca).

Popkin (1990): Jeremy D. Popkin, *Revolutionary News: The Press in France, 1789–1799* (Durham, N.C.).

Popkin (1991): Jeremy D. Popkin, 'The Elite Press in the French Revolution: The Gazette de Leyde and the Gazette Universelle', in Chisick (1991b), pp. 85–98.

Popkin (1993a): Jeremy D. Popkin, 'The Provincial Newspaper Press and Revolutionary Politics', *French Historical Studies*, 18: 434–56.

Popkin (1993b): Jeremy D. Popkin, 'The Business of Political Enlightenment in France, 1770–1800', in John Brewer and Roy Porter (eds) *Consumption and the World of Goods*, pp. 412–36.

Quéniart (1978): Jean Quéniart, *Culture et société urbaine dans la France de l'ouest au XVIIIe siècle* (Paris).

Reichardt (1989): Rolf Reichardt, 'Prints: Images of the Bastille', in Darnton and Roche (1989), pp. 223–51.

Rétat (1979): Pierre Rétat (ed.) *L'Attentat de damiens: discours sur l'événement au XVIIIe siècle* (Paris).

Rétat (1982): Pierre Rétat (ed.) *La Journalisme d'ancien régime: questions et propositions* (Lyons).

Rétat (1985): Pierre Rétat, 'Forme et discours d'un journal révolutionnaire: Les *Révolutions de Paris* en 1789', in Labrosse and Rétat (1985), pp. 139–66.

Rétat (1989): Pierre Rétat, *La Révolution du journal, 1788–1794* (Paris).

Rétat (1993): Pierre Rétat, 'Les Gazetiers de Hollande et les puissances politiques au 18e siècle: une difficile collaboration', *Dix-huitième siècle*, 25: 319–35.

Richet (1991): Denis Richet, 'Les Canaux de la propagation des idées contestaires avant la presse révolutionnaire', in Chisick (1991b), pp. 19–24.

Roche (1978): Daniel Roche, *Le Siècle des lumières en province: académies et académiciens provinciaux, 1680–1789* (Paris).

Roche (1979): Daniel Roche, 'Urban Reading Habits during the French Enlightenment', *British Journal for Eighteenth-Century Studies*, 2: 139–49, 221–31.

Roche (1987): Daniel Roche, *The People of Paris: An Essay in Popular Culture in the Eighteenth Century* (Berkeley).

Sgard (1976): Jean Sgard (ed.) *Dictionnaire de journalistes* (Grenoble).

Sgard (1983): Jean Sgard (ed.) *La Presse provinciale au XVIIIe siècle* (Grenoble).

Sgard (1984): Jean Sgard, 'La Multiplication des périodiques', in Roger Chartier, Henri-Jean Martin and Jean-Pierre Vivet (eds) *Histoire de l'édition française*, vol. 2 (Paris), pp. 198–205.

Sgard (1988): Jean Sgard, 'Les Souscripteurs du *Journal étranger*', in Bots (1988), pp. 89–99.

Sgard (1990): Jean Sgard, 'On dit', in Chisick (1991b), pp. 25–32.

Sgard (1991): Jean Sgard (ed.) *Dictionnaire de journaux, 1600–1789*, 2 vols (Paris).

Soboul (1958): Albert Soboul, *Les Sans-Culottes parisiens de l'an II* (Paris).

Solomon (1972): Howard Solomon, *Public Welfare, Science, and Propaganda in Seventeenth Century France: The Innovations of Théophraste Renaudot* (Princeton).

Tucoo-Chala (1975): Suzanne Tucoo-Chala, *Charles-Joseph Panckoucke et la librairie française, 1736–1798* (Paris).

Van Kley (1984): Dale Van Kley, *The Damiens Affair and the Unraveling of the Ancien Regime, 1750–1770* (Princeton).

Van Kley (1994): Dale Van Kley (ed.) *The French Idea of Freedom: The Old Regime and the Declaration of Rights of 1789* (Stanford, Calif.).

ENGLAND, WALES AND SCOTLAND

Andrew (1989): Donna T. Andrew, *Philanthropy and Police: London Charity in the Eighteenth Century* (Princeton).

Arnot (1779): Hugo Arnot, *The History of Edinburgh* (Edinburgh).

Aspinall (1948): A. Aspinall, 'Statistical Accounts of the London Newspapers during the Eighteenth Century', *English Historical Review*, 63: 201–32.

Aspinall (1949): A. Aspinall, *Politics and the Press c.1780–1850* (1949).

Aspinall (1956): A. Aspinall, 'The Reporting and Publishing of the House of Commons Debates, 1771–1834', in R. Pares and A.J.P. Taylor (eds) *Essays to Sir Lewis Namier*, pp. 227–57.

Asquith (1978): I. Asquith, 'The Structure, Ownership and Control of the Press, 1780–1855', in G. Boyce, J. Curran and P. Wingate, (eds) *Newspaper History from the Seventeenth Century to the Present Day*, pp. 98–116.

Astbury (1978): R. Astbury, 'The Renewal of the Licensing Act in 1693 and its Lapse in 1695', *Library*, 5th ser., 33: 296–322.

Austin (1915): R. Austin, 'Robert Raikes, the Elder, & the Gloucester Journal', *Library*, 3rd ser., 6: 1–24.

Barker (1994): Hannah J. Barker, 'The Press, Politics and Reform, 1779–85', unpublished DPhil thesis, Oxford Unversity.

Barry (1985): Jonathan Barry, 'The Cultural Life of Bristol 1640–1775', unpublished DPhil thesis (Oxford University).

Barry (1991): Jonathan Barry, 'The Press and the Politics of Culture in Bristol 1660–1775', in J. Black and J. Gregory (eds) *Culture, Politics and Society in Britain 1660–1800* (Manchester), pp. 49–81.

Beresford (1926): John Beresford (ed.) *The Diary of a Country Parson: The Reverend James Woodforde* (Oxford).

Black (1986): Jeremy Black, *Natural & Necessary Enemies: Anglo-French Relations in the Eighteenth Century.*

Black (1987a): Jeremy Black, *The English Press in the Eighteenth Century.*

Black (1987b): Jeremy Black, 'An Underrated Journalist: Nathaniel Mist and the Opposition Press during the Whig Ascendancy', *British Journal for Eighteenth-Century Studies*, 10: 27–41.

Black (1988): Jeremy Black, 'George II and the Juries Act: Royal Concern about the Control of the Press', *Historical Research*, 61: 359–62.

Black (1989a): Jeremy Black, 'A Short-Lived Jacobite Newspaper: *The National Journal* of 1746', in Schweizer and Black (1989), pp. 77–88.

Black (1989b): Jeremy Black, 'In Search of a Scandalous Pamphlet: Sir Robert Walpole and the Attempt to Suppress the Publication of Opposition Literature in the United Provinces', *Publishing History*, 25: 5–11.

Black (1991): Jeremy Black, 'Journalism and its Problems in Late Eighteenth-Century England', *Journal of Newspaper and Periodical History*, 7: 31–8.

Black (1993a): Jeremy Black, 'Eighteenth-Century English Politics: Recent Work and Current Problems', *Albion*, xxv: 419–41.

Black (1993b): Jeremy Black, 'Politicisation and the Press in Hanoverian England', in Myers and Harris (1993), pp. 63–81.

Black (1994a): Jeremy Black, *Convergence or Divergence? Britain and the Continent.*

Black (1994b): Jeremy Black, 'Continuity and Change in the British Press 1750–1833', *Publishing History*, 36: 39–85.

Bond and McCleod (1977): D.H. Bond and W.R. McCleod (eds) *Newsletters to Newspapers: Eighteenth-Century Journalism* (Morgantown, W. Va.).

Borsay (1989): Peter Borsay, *The English Urban Renaissance: Culture and Society in the Provincial Town 1660–1770* (Oxford).

Borsay (1994): Peter Borsay, 'The London Connection: Cultural Diffusion and the English Provincial Town', *London Journal*, 19: 21–35.

Brewer (1973): John Brewer, 'The Misfortunes of Lord Bute: A Case Study in Eighteenth-century Political Argument and Public Opinion', *Historical Journal*, 16: 7–43.

Brewer (1976): John Brewer, *Party, Ideology and Popular Politics at the Accession of George III* (Cambridge).

Brewer (1980): John Brewer, 'The Wilkites and the Law, 1763–1774', in John Brewer and John Styles (eds) *An Ungovernable People: The English and their Law in the Seventeenth and Eighteenth Centuries*, pp. 128–71.

Brewer (1982): John Brewer, 'Commercialization and Politics', in N. McKendrick, J. Brewer and J.H. Plumb, *The Birth of a Consumer Society*, pp. 253–60.

Brewer (1983): John Brewer, 'The Number 45: A Wilkite Political Symbol', in S.B. Baxter (ed.) *England's Rise to Greatness, 1660–1763* (Berkeley), pp. 349–80.

Brewer (1989): John Brewer, *The Sinews of Power: War, Money and the English State 1688–1783* (Oxford).

Brown (1975): P.S. Brown, 'The Vendors of Medicines Advertised in Eighteenth-century Bath Newspapers', *Medical History*, 19: 352–69.

Brown (1976): P.S. Brown, 'Medicines Advertised in Eighteenth-century Bath Newspapers,' *Medical History*, 20: 152–68.

Bullion (1989): John Bullion, 'The *Monitor* and the Beer Tax Controversy: A Study of Constraints on London Newspapers of 1760–1761', in Schweizer and Black (1989), pp. 89–117.

Burke (1978): Peter Burke, *Popular Culture in Early Modern Europe*.

Capraro (1984): Rocco Lawrence Capraro, 'Typographic Politics: The Impact of Printing on the Political Life of Eighteenth-century England 1714–1772', unpublished DPhil thesis (Washington University).

Carnie (n.d.): Robert Hay Carnie, 'Provincial Periodical Publishing in Eighteenth-century Scotland: The Dundee Experience', unpublished paper.

Carswell and Dralle (1965): John Carswell and Lewis Arnold Dralle (eds) *The Political Journal of George Bubb Dodington* (Oxford).

Chapman (1983): Paul Chapman, 'Jacobite Political Argument, 1714–1766', unpublished DPhil thesis (Cambridge University).

Christie (1962): I.R. Christie, *Wilkes, Wyvill and Reform: The Parliamentary Reform Movement in British Politics, 1760–1785*.

Christie (1970): I.R. Christie, *Myth and Reality in Late Eighteenth-century British Politics*.

Clark (1985): J.C.D. Clark, *English Society 1688–1832: Ideology, Social Structure and Political Practice during the Ancien Régime* (Cambridge).

Clark (1994): Charles E. Clark, *The Public Prints: The Newspaper in Anglo-American Culture, 1665–1740* (New York and Oxford).

Clive (1970): John Clive, 'The Social Background of the Scottish Renaissance', in N.T. Phillipson and Rosalind Mitchison (eds) *Scotland in the Age of Improvement: Essays in Scottish History in the Eighteenth Century* (Edinburgh), pp. 225–44.

Cobbett (1806–20): William Cobbett (ed.) *The Parliamentary History of England from the Earliest Period to the Year 1803*, 36 vols.

Colley (1981): L. Colley, 'Eighteenth-century English Radicalism before Wilkes', *Transactions of the Royal Historical Society*, 5th ser., 31: 1–19.

Colley (1984): L. Colley, 'The Apotheosis of George III: Loyalty, Royalty and the British Nation 1760–1820', *Past & Present*, 122: 94–129.

Colley (1992): L. Colley, *Britons: Forging of the Nation, 1707–1837* (New Haven, Conn.).

Connolly (1992): S.J. Connolly, *Religion, Law and Power: The Making of Protestant Ireland, 1660–1760* (Oxford).

Cookson (1982): J.E. Cookson, *The Friends of Peace: Anti-War Liberalism in England 1793–1815* (Cambridge).

Cookson (1991): J.E. Cookson, 'The Rise and Fall of the Sutton Volunteers, 1803–4', *Historical Research*, 64: 46–53.

Corfield (1982): Penelope J. Corfield, *The Impact of English Towns 1700–1800* (Oxford).

Corfield (1987): Penelope J. Corfield, 'Class by Name and Number in Eighteenth-century Britain', *History*, 72: 38–61.

Corfield (1991): Penelope J. Corfield (ed.) *Language, History and Class* (Oxford).

Couper (1908): W.J. Couper, *The Edinburgh Periodical Press*, 2 vols (Stirling).

Cowan (1946): R.M.W. Cowan, *The Newspaper in Scotland: A Study of its First Expansion 1815–1860* (Glasgow).

Crafts (1985): N.R.F. Crafts, *Economic Growth during the British Industrial Revolution* (Oxford).

Craig (1931): M.E. Craig, *The Scottish Periodical Press 1750–1789* (Edinburgh).

Cranfield (1962): G.A. Cranfield, *The Development of the Provincial Newspaper, 1700–1760* (Cambridge).

Cranfield (1963): G.A. Cranfield, 'The *London Evening Post*, 1727–1744', *Historical Journal*, 6: 20–37.

Cranfield (1965): G.A. Cranfield, 'The *London Evening Post* and the Jew Bill of 1753', *Historical Journal*, 8: 16–30.

Cranfield (1978): G.A. Cranfield, *The Press and Society: From Caxton to Northcliffe.*

Crawford (1979): Thomas Crawford, *Society and the Lyric: A Study of the Song Culture of Eighteenth-Century Scotland* (Edinburgh).

Cust (1986): Richard Cust, 'News and Politics in Early Seventeenth-century England', *Past & Present*, 112: 60–90.

Davison, Hitchcock, Keirn and Shoemaker (1992): Lee Davison, Tim Hitchcock, Tim Keirn and R.B. Shoemaker (eds) *Stilling the Grumbling Hive: The Response to Social and Economic Problems in England, 1689–1750* (Stroud).

Defoe (1728–9): Daniel Defoe, *The Complete English Tradesmen*, 2 vols, 1745 edn, reprint 1970 (New York).

Devine (1975): T.M. Devine, *The Tobacco Lords: A Study on the Tobacco Merchants of Glasgow and Their Trading Activities, c.1740–90* (Edinburgh).

Devine (1983): T.M. Devine, 'The English Connection and Irish and Scottish Development in the Eighteenth Century', in T.M. Devine and David Dickson (eds) *Ireland and Scotland 1600–1850: Parallels and Contrasts in Economic and Social Development* (Edinburgh), pp. 12–29.

Dickinson (1984): H.T. Dickinson, 'Popular Politics in the Age of Walpole', in J. Black (ed.) *Britain in the Age of Walpole*, pp. 45–68.

Dickinson (1989): H.T. Dickinson, 'Popular Conservatism and Militant Loyalism 1789–1815', in H.T. Dickinson (ed.) *Britain and the French Revolution 1789–1815*, pp. 103–25.

Dickinson (1990): H.T. Dickinson, 'Radicals and Reformers in the Age of Wilkes and Wyvill', in J. Black (ed.) *British Politics and Society from Walpole to Pitt, 1742–1789*, pp. 123–46.

Dickinson (1995): H.T. Dickinson, *The Politics of the People in Eighteenth-century Britain.*

Dickson (1967): P.G.M. Dickson, *The Financial Revolution in England: A Study in the Development of Public Credit, 1688–1756.*

Dinwiddy (1990): John Dinwiddy, 'Conceptions of Revolution in the English Radicalism of the 1790s', in Eckhart Hellmuth (ed.) *The Transformation of Political Culture: England and Germany in the Late Eighteenth Century* (Oxford), pp. 535–60.

Downie (1979): J.A. Downie, *Robert Harley and the Press: Propaganda and Public Opinion in the Age of Swift and Defoe* (Cambridge).

Downie (1981): J.A. Downie, 'The Growth of Government Tolerance of the Press to 1700', in Myers and Harris (1981), pp. 45–50.

Drescher (1994): Seymour Drescher, 'Whose Abolition? Popular Pressure and the Ending of the British Slave Trade', *Past & Present*, 143: 136–66.

Dwyer (1989): John Dwyer, 'The *Caledonian Mercury* and Scottish National Culture, 1763–1801', in Schweizer and Black (1989), pp. 147–69.

Earle (1989): Peter Earle, *The Making of the English Middle Class: Business, Society and Family Life in London, 1660–1730.*

Ellis (1958): Kenneth Ellis, *The Post Office in the Eighteenth Century: A Study in Administrative History* (Oxford).

Emsley (1981): C. Emsley, 'An Aspect of Pitt's "Terror": Prosecutions for Sedition in the 1790s', *Social History*, 6: 155–84.

Emsley (1985): C. Emsley, 'Repression, "Terror" and the Rule of Law in England during the Decade of the French Revolution', *English Historical Review*, 100: 801–25.

Extracts (1965): *Extracts from the Municipal Accounts of Newcastle upon Tyne* (Newcastle).

Eyre-Todd (1931): George Eyre-Todd, *History of Glasgow*, vol. ii., *From the Reformation to the Revolution* (Glasgow).

Fagerstrom (1951): D.I. Fagerstrom, 'The American Revolutionary Movement in Scottish Opinion', unpublished DPhil thesis (Edinburgh University).

Ferdinand (1990): Christine Ferdinand, 'Local Distribution Networks in 18th-century England', in Myers and Harris (1990), pp. 131–49.

Ferdinand (1993): Christine Ferdinand, 'Selling it to the Provinces: News and Commerce round Eighteenth-century Salisbury', in John Brewer and Roy Porter (eds) *Consumption and the World of Goods*, pp. 393–411.

Finn (1993): Margot C. Finn, *After Chartism: Class and Nation in English Radical Politics, 1848–1874* (Cambridge).

Fletcher and Stevenson (1985): Anthony Fletcher and John Stevenson (eds) *Order and Disorder in Early-Modern England* (Cambridge).

Frank (1961): Joseph Frank, *The Beginnings of English Newspapers, 1620–1660* (Cambridge, Mass.).

Fraser (1956): P. Fraser, *The Intelligence of the Secretaries of State and their Monopoly of Licensed News, 1660–1688* (Cambridge).

Frearson (1993): Michael Frearson, 'The Distribution and Readership of London Corantos in the 1620s', in Myers and Harris (1993), pp. 1–26.

Gee (forthcoming): Austin Gee, *The British Volunteer Movement, 1793–1807* (Oxford).

Gibbs (1992): G.C. Gibbs, 'Press and Public Opinion: Prospective', in J.R. Jones, *Liberty Secured? Britain Before and After 1688* (Stanford, Calif.), pp. 231–64.

Green (1985): T.A. Green, *Verdict According to Conscience: Perspectives on the English Criminal Trial Jury, 1200–1800* (Chicago).

Gunn (1983): J.A.W. Gunn, *Beyond Liberty and Property: The Process of Self-recognition in Eighteenth-century Political Thought* (Kingston and Montreal).

Haig (1960): R.L. Haig, *The Gazetteer: 1735–1797* (Carbondale, Ill.)

Haldane (1971): A.D.R. Haldane, *Three Centuries of Scottish Posts: An Historical Survey to 1836* (Edinburgh).

Handover (1965): P.M. Handover, *A History of the London Gazette, 1665–1695.*

Hanson (1936): L. Hanson, *Government and the Press 1695–1763* (Oxford).

Harris (1970): Michael Harris, 'Figures Relating to the Printing and Distribution of the *Craftsman* 1726–1730', *Bulletin of the Institute of Historical Research*, 43: 233–42.

Harris (1978a): Michael Harris, 'The Structure, Ownership and Control of the Press, 1620–1780', in J. Curran, G. Boyce and P. Wingate (eds) *Newspaper History from the Seventeenth Century to the Present Day*, pp. 82–97.

Harris (1978b): Michael Harris, 'The Management of the London Newspaper Press during the Eighteenth Century', *Publishing History*, 4: 95–112.

Harris (1984): Michael Harris, 'Print and Politics in the Age of Walpole', in J. Black (ed.) *Britain in the Age of Walpole*, pp. 189–210.

Harris (1987): Michael Harris, *London Newspapers in the Age of Walpole: A Study in the Origins of the Modern English Press* (London and Toronto).

Harris and Lee (1986): Michael Harris and Alan Lee (eds) *The Press in English Society from the Seventeenth to the Nineteenth Centuries* (London and Toronto).

Robert (Bob) Harris (1993): Robert Harris, *A Patriot Press: National Politics and the London Press in the 1740s* (Oxford).

Harris (1995a): Bob Harris, 'England's Provincial Papers and the Jacobite Rebellion of 1745–6', *History*, 80: 5–21.

Harris (1995b): Bob Harris, '"A Great Palladium of our Liberties": The British Press and the "Forty-Five"', *Historical Research*, 68: 67–87.

Harris (1995c): Bob Harris, 'The *London Evening Post* and Mid-century Politics Revisited', *English Historical Review*, cx: 1132–56.

Harris (1987): Tim Harris, *London Crowds in the Reign of Charles II: Propaganda and Politics from the Restoration until the Exclusion Crisis* (Cambridge).

Harris (1993): Tim Harris, *Politics under the Later Stuarts: Party Conflict in a Divided Society 1660–1715*.

Harrison (1988): Mark Harrison, *Crowds & History: Mass Phenomena in English Towns, 1790–1835* (Cambridge).

Haydon (1993): Colin Haydon, *Anti-Catholicism in Eighteenth-century England c. 1714–80: A Political and Social Study* (Manchester).

Hellmuth (1990): Eckhart Hellmuth, '"The Palladium of All Other English Liberties": Reflections on the Liberty of the Press in England during the 1760s and 1770s', in Eckhart Hellmuth (ed.) *The Transformation of Political Culture: England and Germany* (Oxford), pp. 467–502.

Hobsbawm (1990): Eric Hobsbawm, *Nations and Nationalism since 1780: Programme, Myth, Reality* (Cambridge).

Hodgson (1910): John Crawford Hodgson (ed.) 'The Diary of the Rev. John Tomlinson', *Six North Country Diaries*, Publications of the Surtees Society, cxviii.

Hoppit (1987): Julian Hoppit, *Risk and Failure in English Business 1700–1800* (Cambridge).

Houston (1985): R.A. Houston, *Scottish Literacy and the Scottish Identity: Illiteracy and Society in Scotland and Northern England, 1600–1800* (Cambridge).

Hughes (1956): Edward Hughes (ed.) 'Letters of Spencer Cowper, Dean of Durham 1746–74', *The Publications of the Surtees Society*, clxv.

Hyland (1986): P.B.J. Hyland, 'Liberty and Libel: Government and the Press during the Succession Crisis in Britain, 1712–1716', *English Historical Review*, 101: 875–88.

Innes (1990): J. Innes, 'Parliament and the Shaping of Eighteenth-century English Social Policy', *Transactions of the Royal Historical Society*, 40: 63–92.

Jenkins (1983): Philip Jenkins, *The Making of a Ruling Class: The Glamorgan Gentry 1640–1790* (Cambridge).

Jones (1961): J.R. Jones, *The First Whigs: The Politics of the Exclusion Crisis, 1678–83* (Oxford).

Jordan and Rogers (1989): Gerald Jordan and Nicholas Rogers, 'Admirals as Heroes: Patriotism and Liberty in Hanoverian England', *Journal of British Studies*, xxviii: 201–24.

Kelsall and Kelsall (1986): Helen and Keith Kelsall, 'How People and News Got Around', in *Scottish Life Style 300 Years Ago: New Light on Edinburgh and Border Families* (Edinburgh), pp. 107–24.

Kidd (1993): Colin Kidd, *Subverting Scotland's Past: Scottish Whig Historians and the Creation of an Anglo-British Identity, 1689–c.1830* (Cambridge).

King (1989): Peter King, 'Prosecution Associations and their Impact in Eighteenth-century Essex', in Douglas Hay and Francis G. Snyder, *Policing and Prosecution in Britain, 1750–1850* (Oxford), pp. 171–207.

Knights (1994): Mark Knights, 'Politics and Opinion during the Exclusion Crisis, 1678–81', unpublished DPhil thesis (Oxford University).

Knox (1979): T.R. Knox, 'Popular Politics and Provincial Radicalism: Newcastle upon Tyne, 1769–1785', *Albion*, 11: 220–39.

Kropf (1974–5): C.R. Kropf, 'Libel and Satire in the Eighteenth Century', *Eighteenth-Century Studies*, 8: 153–68.

Lambert (1992): Sheila Lambert, 'Coranto Printing in England: The First Newsbooks', *Journal of Newspaper and Periodical History*, 8: 3–19.

Langford (1975): Paul Langford, *The Excise Crisis: Society and Politics in the Age of Walpole* (Oxford).

Langford (1989): Paul Langford, *A Polite and Commercial People: England 1727–1783* (Oxford).

Langford (1991): Paul Langford, *Public Life and the Propertied Englishmen 1689–1798* (Oxford).

Levy (1982): F.J. Levy, 'How Information Spread among the Gentry, 1550–1640', *Journal of British Studies*, xxi: 11–34.

Lewis (1948): W.S. Lewis (ed.) 'Horace Walpole's Short Notes', in *The Yale Edition of Horace Walpole's Correspondence* (New Haven, Conn.).

Lindert and Williamson (1982): Peter H. Lindert and Jeffrey G. Williamson, 'Revising England's Social Tables 1688–1812', *Explorations in Economic History*, 19: 384–408.

Logue (1979): K.J. Logue, *Popular Disturbances in Scotland 1780–1815* (Edinburgh).

Looney (1989): J.J. Looney, 'Cultural Life in the Provinces: Leeds and York, 1770–1820', in A.L. Beier, David Cannadine and James Rosenheim (eds) *The First Modern Society: Essays in English History in Honour of Lawrence Stone* (Cambridge), pp. 483–510.

Low and Low (1889–90): James G. Low and W. Low, 'Bibliography of Montrose Periodical Literature', *Scottish Notes and Queries*, 1889: 5, 23, 40, 57, 74, 88, 96; 1890: 55.

Lowe (1988): W.C. Lowe, 'Peers and Printers: The Beginnings of Sustained Press Coverage of the House of Lords in the 1770s', *Parliamentary History*, 7: 241–56.

Lutnick (1967): S. Lutnick, *The American Revolution and the British Press, 1775–1783* (Columbia, Mo.).

Manuscripts (1920–3): *Manuscripts of the Earl of Egmont, Diary of Viscount Percival, afterwards First Earl of Egmont*, 3 vols, Historical Manuscripts Commission.

McKendrick (1982): Neil McKendrick, 'Josiah Wedgewood and the Commercialization of the Potteries', in Neil McKendrick, John Brewer and J.H. Plumb (eds) *The Birth of a Consumer Society*, pp. 100–45.

Mather (1992): F.C. Mather, *High Church Prophet: Bishop Samuel Horsley and the Caroline Tradition in the Later Georgian Church* (Oxford).

Maxted (1990): Ian Maxted, 'Single Sheets from a County Town: Exeter', in Myers and Harris (1990), pp. 109–29.

Meikle (1912): Henry W. Meikle, *Scotland and the French Revolution* (Edinburgh).

Mitchell (1987): C.J. Mitchell, 'Provincial Printing in Eighteenth-century Britain', *Publishing History*, xxi: 5–24.

Money (1971): J. Money, 'Taverns, Coffee Houses and Clubs: Local Politics and Popular Articulacy in the Birmingham Area in the Age of the American Revolution', *Historical Journal*, 14: 15–47.

Money (1977): J. Money, *Experience and Identity: Birmingham and the West Midlands 1760–1800* (Manchester).

Money (1993): J. Money, 'The Masonic Moment; Or, Ritual, Replica, and Credit: John Wilkes, the Macaroni Parson, and the Making of the Middle-Class Mind', *Journal of British Studies*, 32: 358–95.

Monod (1989): Paul Kléber Monod, *Jacobitism and the English People, 1688–1788* (Cambridge).

Mori (1992): J.C. Mori, 'The Impact of the French Revolution on the Ideas and Policies of William Pitt, 1789–1795', unpublished DPhil thesis (Oxford University).

Myers and Harris (1981): Robin Myers and Michael Harris (eds) *The Development of the English Book Trade, 1700–1793* (Oxford).

Myers and Harris (1990): Robin Myers and Michael Harris (eds) *Spreading the Word: The Distribution Networks of Print 1550–1850* (Winchester and St Paul).

Myers and Harris (1993): Robin Myers and Michael Harris (eds) *Serials and their Readers 1620–1914* (Winchester).

Nenadic (1988): Stana Nenadic, 'The Rise of the Urban Middle Class', in T.M. Devine and Rosalind Mitchison (eds) *People and Society in Scotland: Volume 1, 1760–1830* (Edinburgh), pp. 109–26.

Nenadic (1990): Stana Nenadic, 'Political Reform and the "Ordering" of Middle-Class Protest', in T.M. Devine (ed.) *Conflict and Stability in Scottish Society 1700–1850* (Edinburgh), pp. 65–82.

Newman (1987): Gerald Newman, *The Rise of English Nationalism: A Cultural History 1740–1830*.

O'Gorman (1989): Frank O'Gorman, *Voters, Patrons and Parties: The Unreformed Electorate of Hanoverian England, 1734–1832* (Oxford).

Oldham (1983): J.C. Oldham, 'The Origins of the Special Jury', *University of Chicago Law Review*, 50: 177–221.

Olson (1979–80): Alison G. Olson, 'The Board of Trade and London–American

Interest Groups in the Eighteenth Century', *Journal of Imperial and Commonwealth History*, 8: 33–50.

Pawson (1977): Eric Pawson, *Transport and Economy: The Turnpike Roads of Eighteenth-century Britain.*

Perry (1962): T.W. Perry, *Public Opinion, Propaganda and Politics in Eighteenth-century England: A Study of the Jewish Naturalization Act of 1753* (Cambridge, Mass.).

Peters (1980): M. Peters, *Pitt and Popularity: The Patriot Minister and London Opinion during the Seven Years War* (Oxford).

Phillips (1982): J.A. Phillips, *Electoral Behaviour in Unreformed England: Plumpers, Splitters, and Straights* (Princeton).

Phillipson (1970): N.T. Phillipson, 'Scottish Public Opinion and the Union in the Age of Association', in N.T. Phillipson and Rosalind Mitchison (eds) *Scotland in the Age of Improvement* (Edinburgh), pp. 125–47.

Plumb (1968): J.H. Plumb, 'Political Man', in James L. Clifford (ed.) *Man versus Society in Eighteenth-century Britain* (Cambridge).

Porter (1990): Roy Porter, 'Science, Provincial Culture and Public Opinion in Enlightenment England', in Peter Borsay (ed.) *The Eighteenth-century Town: A Reader in English Urban History, 1688–1820*, pp. 243–67.

Pottle (1951): Frederick A. Pottle (ed.) *Boswell's London Journal, 1762–1763.*

Price (1958): J.M. Price, 'A Note on the Circulation of the London Press, 1704–1714', *Bulletin of the Institute of Historical Research*, 31: 215–19.

Price (1983): J.M. Price, 'The Excise Affair Revisited: The Administrative and Colonial Dimensions of a Parliamentary Crisis', in Stephen B. Baxter (ed.) *England's Rise to Greatness 1660–1763* (Los Angeles and London), pp. 257–321.

Raven (1993): James Raven, 'Serial Advertisement in 18th Century Britain and Ireland', in Myers and Harris (1993), pp. 103–22.

Raymond (1993): Joad Raymond (ed.) *Making the News: An Anthology of the Newsbooks of Revolutionary England, 1641–1660* (New York and London).

Rea (1963): R.R. Rea, *The English Press in Politics, 1760–1774* (Lincoln, Nebr.).

Read (1961): Donald Read, *Press and People 1790–1850: Opinion in Three English Cities.*

Reeves and Morrison (1988): Marjorie Reeves and Jean Morrison (eds) 'The Diaries of Jeffrey Whitaker, Schoolmaster of Bratton, 1739–41', *Publications of Wiltshire Record Society*, xliv.

Rogers (1989): Nicholas Rogers, *Whigs and Cities: Popular Politics in the Age of Walpole and Pitt* (Oxford).

Sack (1993): J.J. Sack, *From Jacobite to Conservative: Reaction and Orthodoxy in Britain c.1760–1832* (Cambridge).

Schaaber (1965): M.A. Schaaber, *Some Forerunners of the Newspaper in England 1476–1776* (Urbana, Ill.).

Schweizer (1988): Karl Schweizer, 'Lord Bute and the Press: The Origins of the Press War of 1762 Reconsidered', in Karl Schweizer (ed.) *Lord Bute: Essays in Re-interpretation* (Leicester).

Schweizer and Black (1989): Karl Schweizer and Jeremy Black (eds) *Politics and the Press in Hanoverian Britain* (Lewiston).

Schweizer and Klein (1989): Karl Schweizer and Rebecca Klein, 'The French Revolution and Developments in the London Daily Press to 1793', in Schweizer and Black (1989), pp. 171–86.

Schwoerer (1979): Lois Schwoerer, 'Press and Parliament in the Revolution of 1688', *Historical Journal*, 20: 545–67.

Siebert (1965): F.S. Siebert, *Freedom of the Press in England 1476–1776* (Urbana, Ill.).

Smail (1994): John Smail, *The Origins of Middle-class Culture: Halifax, Yorkshire, 1660–1780* (Ithaca).

Smith (1979): M.J. Smith, 'English Radical Newspapers in the French Revolutionary Era, 1790–1803', unpublished DPhil thesis (University of London).

Smout (1989): T.C. Smout, 'Problems of Nationalism, Identity and Improvement in Later Eighteenth-century Scotland', in T.M. Devine (ed.) *Improvement and Enlightenment: Proceedings of the Scottish Historical Studies Seminar, University of Strathclyde, 1987–8* (Edinburgh), pp. 1–21.

Snyder (1968): Henry Snyder, 'The Circulation of Newspapers in the Reign of Queen Anne', *Library*, 5th ser., 23: 206–21.

Snyder (1976): Henry Snyder, 'A Further Note on the Circulation of Newspapers in the Reign of Queen Anne', *Library*, 5th ser., 31: 387–9.

Speck (1972): W.A. Speck, 'Political Propaganda in Augustan England', *Transactions of the Royal Historical Society*, 5th ser., 22: 17–32.

Spufford (1985): M. Spufford, *Small Books and Pleasant Histories: Popular Fiction and its Readership in Seventeenth Century England* (Cambridge).

Stone and Stone (1984): Lawrence Stone and Jeanne C. Fawtier Stone, *An Open Elite? England 1540–1880* (Oxford).

Styles (1993): John Styles, 'Manufacturing, Consumption and Design in Eighteenth-century England', in John Brewer and Roy Porter (eds) *Consumption and the World of Goods*, pp. 527–54.

Sutherland (1986): James Sutherland, *The Restoration Newspaper and its Development* (Cambridge).

Swinfen (1976): David Swinfen, 'The American Revolution in the Scottish Press', in O. Edwards and G. Shepperson (eds) *Scotland, Europe and the American Revolution* (Edinburgh), pp. 66–74.

Targett (1989): Simon Targett, 'A Pro-government Newspaper during the Whig Ascendancy: Walpole's *London Journal*, 1722–1738', in Schweizer and Black (1989), pp. 1–32.

Targett (1991): Simon Targett, 'Sir Robert Walpole's Newspapers 1722–42: Propaganda and Politics in the Age of Whig Supremacy', unpublished DPhil thesis (Cambridge University).

Thomas (1982): J.P. Thomas, 'The British Empire and the Press 1763–1774', unpublished DPhil thesis (Oxford University).

Thomas (1959): P.D.G. Thomas, 'The Beginning of Parliamentary Reporting in the Newspapers, 1768–1774', *English Historical Review*, 74: 623–36.

Thomas (1960): P.D.G. Thomas, 'John Wilkes and the Freedom of the Press', *Bulletin of the Institute of Historical Research*, 33: 86–98.

Thompson (1991): E.P. Thompson, *Customs in Common*.

Vaisey (1986): David Vaisey (ed.) *The Diary of Thomas Turner, 1754–1765*.

Varey (1982): Simon Varey (ed.) *Lord Bolingbroke's Contributions to the Craftsman* (Oxford).

Wahrman (1992a): Dror Wahrman, 'National Society, Communal Culture: An Argument about the Recent Historiography of Eighteenth-century Britain', *Social History*, 17: 43–72.

Wahrman (1992b): Dror Wahrman, 'Virtual Representation: Parliamentary Reporting and Languages of Class in the 1790s', *Past & Present*, 136: 83–113.

Walker (1973): R.B. Walker, 'Advertising in London Newspapers, 1650–1750', *Business History*, 15: 112–30.

Walker (1974): R.B. Walker, 'The Newspaper Press in the Reign of William III', *Historical Journal*, 17: 691–709.

Watt (1981): Tessa Watt, *Cheap Print and Popular Piety, 1550–1640* (Cambridge).

Wells (1988): Roger Wells, *Wretched Faces: Famine in Wartime England 1793–1801* (Gloucester and New York).

Werkmeister (1963): L. Werkmeister, *The London Daily Press, 1772–1792* (Lincoln, Nebr.).

Werkmeister (1967): L. Werkmeister, *A Newspaper History of England, 1792–1793* (Lincoln, Nebr.).

Wigley (1975): J. Wigley, 'James Montgomery and the *Sheffield Iris*, 1792–1825: A Study in the Weakness of Provincial Radicalism', *Transactions of the Hunter Archaeological Society*, 10: 173–81.

Wiles (1965): R.M. Wiles, *Freshest Advices: Early Provincial Newspapers in England* (Columbia).

Wiles (1976): R.M. Wiles, 'The Relish for Reading in Provincial England Two Centuries Ago', in P.J. Korshin (ed.) *The Widening Circle: Essays on the Circulation of Literature in Eighteenth Century Europe* (Philadelphia), pp. 87–105.

Wilson (1988): K. Wilson, 'Empire, Trade and Popular Politics in Mid-Hanoverian Britain: The Case of Admiral Vernon', *Past & Present*, 121: 74–109.

Wilson (1992): K. Wilson, 'A Dissident Legacy: Eighteenth Century Popular Politics and the Glorious Revolution', in J.R. Jones (ed.) *Liberty Secured? Britain Before and After 1688* (Stanford, Calif.), pp. 299–334, 387–93.

Wilson (1986): Richard Wilson, 'Newspapers and Industry: The Export of Wool Controversy in the 1780s', in Harris and Lee (1986), pp. 80–104.

Wilson (1822): Robert Wilson, *An Historical Account and Delineation of Aberdeen* (Aberdeen).

Winkler (1988): K.T. Winkler, 'The Forces of the Market and the London Newspaper in the First Half of the Eighteenth Century', *Journal of Newspaper and Periodical History*, 4: 22–35.

Wood and Armet (1954): M. Wood and H. Armet (eds) *Extracts from the Records of the Burgh of Edinburgh 1681 to 1689* (Edinburgh and London).

Wrightson and Levine (1991): Keith Wrightson and David Levine, *The Making of an Industrial Society: Whickham, 1560–1765* (Oxford).

Name index

Subject index